DIVORCE

Reclaiming your identity

JOHN MICHAEL GIBSON

Divorcing Divorce

Trilogy Christian Publishers

A Wholly Owned Subsidiary of Trinity Broadcasting Network

2442 Michelle Drive

Tustin, CA 92780

Copyright © 2024 by John Michael Gibson

Scripture quotations marked NIV are taken from the Holy Bible, New International Version®, NIV®. Copyright © 1973, 1978, 1984, 2011 by Biblica, Inc.™ Used by permission of Zondervan. All rights reserved worldwide. www.zondervan.com. The "NIV" and "New International Version" are trademarks registered in the United States Patent and Trademark Office by Biblica, Inc.™

Scripture quotations marked KJV are taken from the King James Version of the Bible. Public domain.

All rights reserved, including the right to reproduce this book or portions thereof in any form whatsoever.

For information, address Trilogy Christian Publishing

Rights Department, 2442 Michelle Drive, Tustin, CA 92780.

Trilogy Christian Publishing/ TBN and colophon are trademarks of Trinity Broadcasting Network.

For information about special discounts for bulk purchases, please contact Trilogy Christian Publishing.

Trilogy Disclaimer: The views and content expressed in this book are those of the author and may not necessarily reflect the views and doctrine of Trilogy Christian Publishing or the Trinity Broadcasting Network.

10 9 8 7 6 5 4 3 2 1

Library of Congress Cataloging-in-Publication Data is available.

ISBN: 979-8-89041-937-8

ISBN: 979-8-89041-938-5

Table of Contents

INTRODUCTION 1

CHAPTER ONE: 3

CHAPTER TWO: 13

CHAPTER THREE: 26

CHAPTER FOUR: 36

CHAPTER FIVE: 45

CHAPTER SIX: 62

CHAPTER SEVEN: 72

CHAPTER EIGHT: 83

CHAPTER NINE: 94

CHAPTER TEN: 104

CONCLUSION 111

INTRODUCTION

To be honest, I have always hated reading introductions to books. I personally think they are a bit pointless, being that you have most likely, subconsciously, already made a decision to read this book. Maybe the title intrigued you just enough to click the buy button online or to reach out and grab it in person. Maybe it was the snippet on the back that told what you'd find inside. Either way, your mind is pretty much made up. So, why then should I write an entire chapter encouraging you, or explaining to you, what you are about to already read. I mean just in these few seconds of my rant of hating introductions I think we can both agree we want to get to the point. We want to get to healing. We want to get to a place of hope. We want to get to the other side and finally "Divorce Divorce." So here is the introduction:

Divorcees

If you are reading this and you have been through divorce, this book is going to transform your life. I personally believe that you will never read anything as raw, real, and open on a topic of this magnitude. So, buckle up. You will be confronted with your past. You will be challenged to change. Your pain will resurface. Your own memories will begin to captivate you. However, this is not a bad thing. This is all part of the process of what needs to happen when truly overcoming the identity of being divorced. That is why I've titled this book divorcing divorce. Because many of you reading this need to finally divorce your divorce!

You need to finally accept it, move on, and walk in the freedom God has for you. It is time for your identity to be reestablished in Christ. Through that you will finally be able to live with purpose again!

Non-Divorcees

If you are reading this and you haven't been divorced, I have to say this, you don't understand. You can be a pastor with all the Bible knowledge in the world, and you don't understand. You can have a doctorate on divorce, and I promise, you don't understand. You can be the best psychologist in the world, having done thousands of counseling sessions with divorcees, but you don't understand. It doesn't matter if you are a child that had parents get divorced and you were there for every moment, the truth is, you weren't. They protected you from things that could have caused so much more damage than already done. The truth is, the only way to understand divorce, is by having been through one! So here is what I am asking you. Read this with an open heart. Read this with an open mind. There are going to be things you read that maybe you had never heard before. Maybe you never thought about them. I hope that after reading this though, it guides you into a deeper understanding of what your divorced church members, friends, family members, sons, daughters, or parents might be going through. I hope this book helps you in the future to better walk with those going through a divorce and not distance yourself from them!

CHAPTER ONE:

DECISION DAY

I will never forget the day I first laid eyes on her. Not the first day I had seen her, but the first day I *really laid eyes* on her. It was at 10:00 a.m. on Monday morning. I was sitting in my newly assigned chapel seat at the Christian University I was attending. It was the beginning semester of my senior year. As I took my seat in the back left corner of the chapel I looked up, and she caught my eye. Keep in mind I had seen her before, but I never noticed her like I did today. As she walked down the aisle to take her seat, only a few rows in front of me there was a glow surrounding her. Her black dress swayed as she walked past, gold earrings glimmering in the light. I could hear the sound of her high heels as they passed by me. I couldn't keep my eyes off of her as she made her way to her seat. This girl was absolutely beautiful. I am sure I was not the only guy that noticed her that day, but I had a leg up on all the competition. I remembered we had previously had a class together early in our college careers that allowed me to obtain her phone number. I quickly pulled out my cell phone to send a short text, not even sure if she still had my number. You could say I was being pretty pathetic at the time. Looking back, I have no idea why I threw myself at her like a young boy who had never even seen a girl before. I had been in plenty relationships and if I were honest, most of the time, I was the one being pursued.

However, this time, things were different. The text I sent went something like this, "Now you know better than to be walking in a chapel service looking like that." Let me stop right here before you all go judging me by saying, "You are supposed to be a preacher, why are you lusting in chapel?" First of all, the spirit was not lust, it was mere over-infatuation. Second, I was a twenty-two-year-old kid, so leave me alone. After sending the text, I waited for what seemed like days for a response. I am sure it was only about three minutes total but at the time it felt like a lifetime. Finally! My phone vibrated! As nervous as I was and as pathetic as I had already been, I decided to play it cool and not text back immediately. So, I waited a whole thirty seconds. I tried to put on my, what I thought to be at the time, charm. How do you do that through text message? I still have no idea. Nonetheless, we texted back and forth for a few moments before chapel began and our conversation came to an abrupt halt at the sound of the worship team beginning to play, triggering the moment all cell phones were to be put away.

That moment plays over and over in my mind as I think back to the first time I really laid eyes on her. You could say it was the beginning of the most life-altering season of my young adult life. Of course, at the time I thought it was the start of a lifetime together. The irony of starting off a relationship with a simple text is insurmountable, but we will get to that part later. Fast forward three years and three months to another day I will never forget. It was November 21, 2015. The day started off like any other day in the life of a young married couple. I had awoken to the sound of that same woman's feet, now my wife, walking around in the bathroom of our newly purchased, big, two-story house. I heard the hair dryer going as she prepared herself for a ministry outing we had that day, at least that is what I thought. We had committed to serving a Thanksgiving meal to those in the community who may not have one. The outing was going to be taking place at our church that afternoon where I was on staff. As I got out of the bed, I walked into the bathroom to take a shower. I kissed my wife good morning and went about my business. Once my shower was over, I walked out to an unexpected scene. My normal morning had taken an unexpected shift in a different direction.

The once thought to be a day of ministry turned into what would later be described as a day of misery. My wife was seated at the edge of the bed with a small bag packed and the smell of the green beans she had made the night before filled the air. She was in tears. Much to my surprise she was not preparing to go to the Thanksgiving meal. Instead, she looked at me with tear filled eyes and explained that she needed to go home to see her family for a few days. She had the green beans ready for me to take to the meal, but she would not be attending. I thought nothing of the venture home at the time and even encouraged it. We had recently moved a couple hours away from her family so that I could take a job in full-time ministry. I knew she was very close with her family, and the move was taking its toll on her. Part of the agreement of moving was that she would be able to go home anytime she needed. So of course, that morning I supported her decision to go spend time with her family. Little did I know that would be the last time I would see, or hear my wife's voice, until the day I was taking the stand at a divorce mediation hearing.

As the weekend came to an end and the weekdays began, there was still no sign of my wife. Day after day I would call and text wondering what was going on and wondering why she was not answering my phone calls. A week went by of not seeing her. The only communication we had was through text messaging. Here is the irony I was telling you about. I used to joke that

Divorcing Divorce

I am probably the only person to have begun a marriage, and have one ended, through text. Anyway, you have heard the term, "emotional roller coaster?" Well, consider my roller coaster to have been the largest, fastest, scariest roller coaster of my twenty-five-year-old young-adult life. So many thoughts and questions filled my head. *Why was she not responding? Why would she not come home? Why would she not answer her phone? Does this mean we are separated? Does this mean we are getting a divorce? How could God do this to me?* So many questions and no answers.

Thanksgiving came and went. Still no sign of my wife coming home. I spent our two-year anniversary alone in our newly purchased, big, two-story house that I once imagined being filled with a family of my own. Christmas that year was a real hoot as well. Out of fear of what people would say, and not wanting to answer my family's questions about where my wife was, I decided to spend the holiday alone in what was becoming *my lonely,* newly purchased, big, two-story house. My long exasperating text messages to my wife filled with righteous anger and emotions went from aimless rambling to a simple one liner, "I love you, come home." It was not long after Christmas I had to face my greatest fear that had been looming in the back of my mind since the day she did not return. I received the most painstaking text message I had ever received.

Once again, the irony. It read, "I do not want to be married anymore." Yep, this was it. I was twenty-five years old and on my way to being a divorced pastor. I would joke that being a twenty-five-year-old divorced pastor had a nice ring to it, plus I had tattoos and earrings to top it off. As you can tell, joking was my way of coping because it was honestly the worst thing I had ever faced in my life, and I had been through some tough experiences.

While going through this traumatic season of life, all I could do is replay that moment that I first laid eyes on her in the chapel of our Christian University. How could this once stunningly beautiful woman turn into the person I now saw in my eyes. How could the girl that I stood beside at the altar with and gave my life to in a covenant marriage now decide she didn't want to be with me? What had I done to push her to that point? Was it my fault? Was something wrong with me? Those are all the questions that I battled for years after my divorce. Was I just really unlovable or was God somehow punishing me for all the people I hurt in my past? No relationship I was ever in worked out. Mainly because I would break them off right at the time of full commitment. Yet, with her I went all in. What happened? Looking back, now that I have grown in maturity, I know what happened. The truth is that we did not study each other enough before we decided to get married.

Like many young kids that enter into marriage we merely focused on the outside appearance of each other and neglected all the red flags that would hinder us from having a fruitful marriage. We never took the time to ask the tough questions because, like many people, we knew the answers would not point toward marriage, so we ignored them. She was a girl that loved her family and valued every moment with them. She never had plans of leaving her hometown or her family behind. I was a young boy driven by dreams of taking on the world through preaching the gospel. I wanted to do ministry and I was prepared to go wherever God would call me, no matter the distance. That alone would have told us that we were not right for each other. Yet, like all young kids getting married, we had figured it out. There was absolutely nothing you could do to stop us. Am I saying God wanted a divorce for us simply because we did not study each other? No, that is not what I am saying. Let me make myself clear, I do not ever believe God allows people to get married because He for some unforeseeable reason wants them to later get divorced. Divorce tears the very fabric of God's heart. However, we do have to be honest sometimes and realize that God does not call us into a marriage, He simply created marriage for our enjoyment to bring glory to Himself. Who you choose to marry is up to you. I believe God gives us something called, "Free Will." What I am saying is that our divorce was simply because of our choices and mistakes, not God's. I also want to say I do not blame the divorce on her nor do I blame it on God. If anybody is to blame in the situation it would be me for not taking the time to study the woman that I was going to enter into a lifelong relationship with. Yes, she did hurt me. Yes, she did walk out. However, I cannot cast all the blame on her. Marriage is 100/100. Each party is fully responsible for making the marriage a success and fully responsible if the marriage fails. We can all look back and see things that we could have done differently. Like they say, hindsight is 20/20. For everything she did wrong I am sure, actually scratch those last two words, *I know*, I did just as many things wrong. I realize that my divorce experience is not the same as everyone else's. However, I know that regardless of how the divorce came to pass, we all have to take our portion. If I stood here today and continued to cast blame rather than take my full portion, I would not have been able to divorce the divorce and write this book. You say, "What do you mean divorce the divorce?" When I say we need to "divorce divorce" I mean divorcing the things that Satan tries to hold over us or put in our minds after the marital divorce. The bitterness, unforgiveness, loneliness, rejection, sadness, distrust, unworthiness, and anything else he can use to trap you in bondage.

Decision Day

Going through a divorce is never easy. It doesn't matter who you are or which side of the divorce you are on. If you have ever been through one, you understand. That is the only way to put it, *you understand*. There are so many things that happen during a divorce that I would never wish on my worst enemy. The loneliness you feel deep inside cannot be resolved by any amount of friends you have trying to get you out of the house. The distrust that looms in the mind after having gone through such a tragic experience cannot be regained overnight. Sometimes, it takes years. Even the rat race of trying to hide the fact that you are keeping everybody in your life at an arm's distance so they cannot hurt you can be so exhausting. Especially since many of the people you push away just want to help you. NO! I would never wish divorce on anybody, not even my worst enemy. I am sure if you were honest, whether you have experienced a divorce personally or have been a child caught in the middle of your parents' divorce, you feel the same way.

Divorce sucks! It sucks bad! So, the question is what are we going to do about it? I am not writing this book in hopes that some magic words jump off the page and change your life. I am also not writing this book for you to read and justify getting a divorce. If you are on that path, I hope this chapter alone scares the hell out of you so much that you don't ever consider divorce again. You don't want it! I am writing this book for those who have been through a divorce, or who are going through a divorce, to help them to remove the label they have adopted from Satan. I hope to share from my personal experience with divorce to show you that the enemy wants to use the label of divorce against you the rest of your life if you will let him. That is right! I said if you will let him. Today you have a choice. You can continue to live in the misery of a failed marriage the rest of your life. You can wake up every morning, put that scarlet letter of divorce around your neck, walk outside thinking everybody knows, and let the enemy defeat you day after day. Or you can do something different. You can finally say you have had enough of self-loathing for one lifetime, admit things didn't work, and begin *Divorcing Divorce*. It's "Decision Day," what are you going to do?

CHAPTER ONE GROWTH PLAN

1. Identify what hurts you the most about being divorced?

2. What part of the divorce do you blame on your ex-spouse?

3. An even tougher question; what part of the divorce do you blame yourself?

4. Identify and list what you need to forgive yourself for doing and what you need to forgive your ex-spouse for doing before, during, or after the divorce?

5. What does divorcing divorce mean to you?

CHAPTER TWO:

DISHES DON'T WASH THEMSELVES

I wish I could say with as much enthusiasm as chapter one ended, that in one day I made a decision to *Divorce Divorce* and everything changed. Sorry to be a buzzkill but that didn't happen. It was a process. I will not sugar coat it. The process was long, painful, but worth it. In the midst of this process, I coined a phrase over my life, "dishes don't wash themselves." It came about one day after friends of mine came over to see how I was doing. Their ultimate goal was to get me out of the house so that I would not continue to commit mental suicide by spending all my time alone. When they came in, they found me persistently washing dishes. They tried to convince me that I needed to get out of the house and that I needed to be social. I didn't have time to come up with a great excuse, so I said, "I can't do it, dishes don't wash themselves."

At that moment, I had no idea the power those words would have over my life. I had no idea the depth they would travel in my soul. I had no idea the damage they would do. You say how could a simple statement like, "dishes don't wash themselves" do so much harm? Well, it wasn't so much the statement, as much as what the statement represented. Saying, "dishes don't wash themselves" was me saying that life must go on. I would tell myself that life was not going to stop because of my pain so

I just needed to keep going, stay busy, and get over it. I had to keep my head up and keep moving because things will not get done on their own, "dishes don't wash themselves ya know?" What that creed did was give me an excuse to not face my feelings. I utilized it as justification to stay busy and never really process my true emotions. Let's face it, men and emotion don't go hand in hand. Instead of dealing with my feelings, I actually began to have myself fooled that I was doing okay. I knew as long as I stayed busy, stayed consistent, and buried my head in whatever had my attention in the moment, I would be just fine. However, that is not how the process of emotions work. Instead, I ended up emotionally running myself into the ground. It was on the back of my creed that my pride led to my own mental breakdown. It was my pride that said I don't need help. It was my pride that told me to push my feelings down. It was my pride that kept me busy.

Some of you today are doing the same thing. You have jumped back into life and never allowed yourself to process your emotions. The process of dealing with the real-life questions and pain that you are experiencing is not fun, but it is necessary. I found out the hard way that processing is not optional. It is only a matter of time before the ugly box of emotions gets too full and the lid cannot be contained. Eventually, those emotions spew out, revealing all that you have worked so hard to conceal. My hope is to help you to deal with your emotions before your emotional box explodes like mine did. One thing I believe that helps to unpack our emotions is to understand that they are normal. Even more so, they are from God. In this chapter, I am going to share the deepest, darkest, emotional time in my life. I'm willing to do this on the hunch that I am not the only person that handled or is handling their emotions in an unhealthy manner.

The next several pages you will read about exactly how I handled myself during my divorce. I am in no way condoning my actions or the way I responded to all the emotions that came with my divorce. I am only hoping that as I share my story, and the stages of grief that I experienced, you will realize you are not alone in your feelings. As a matter of fact, my prayer is that if you find that you are in one of these places you will admit it to yourself now without having to go through all that I did to find healing. This is simply an opportunity to let you in on the real-life feelings, and even failures, of somebody that knows where you are and has been through what you are going through. So, without judgment, let's take a look at the stages of grief I experienced. Now these are in no way "scientific" but maybe you can relate.

Disbelief

Whether you saw divorce coming from a mile away or it just seemed to come out of nowhere, I imagine disbelief was somewhere in your box of emotions. It was definitely in my box. That was the first of many feelings that began to engulf my life. The day my wife told me she no longer wanted to be married was really a moment of disbelief. Not because I was some perfect husband that did everything right. I wasn't and didn't. Like many of you, I figured no matter how bad it got, we would always work through it. So, disbelief came because I didn't get married with the intention of ever getting a divorce. As a Christian, "divorce was not an option." I would go on a limb here to say that none of you reading this book got married with the intention of getting a divorce. So, when divorce happens, disbelief is a common emotion for all who are involved. That includes, spouses, kids, family members, friends, and even co-workers. Divorce affects more than just those signing the papers.

That is where many of you are today. You are in a state of disbelief. Regardless of how the divorce came about (adultery, abuse, abandonment, love lost, etc.) there are still so many questions that flood your mind every day. How can all the time and love that has been invested be thrown away? How could the one person I trusted my life to, in what I considered to still be for a lifetime, decide they no longer want to be with me? What led to this? Why is this happening to me? How could they do this to our family? How could they do this to our kids? Not to mention, what does it mean for my faith and my relationship with God? Why would God let this happen to me if He is in control? There are so many questions that follow the realization and disbelief of having to face divorce. I have no idea what your questions are, how difficult they are, or anti-religious they are. However, I do know that it is perfectly okay and understandable to question during this time. You will do a lot of questioning God during this process. God is not intimidated or bothered by your questions. Throughout the Bible, we see great men and women of faith question God. Not only do we see them question God, but we see God remain faithful to them. One thing we must remember, even in times of disbelief, is that God will never leave you or forsake you. Even when we cannot see Him or when we don't understand what He is doing, our hope is in His love for us.

I'm Fine

After getting over the initial shock of divorce, I moved into another phase. This was more of a defensive, tough guy, "I'm fine" phase. It is quite common for people to turn to all sorts of things when dealing with a difficult situation. People turn to drugs, food, alcohol, other people, or a multitude of substances, objects, or tasks. Whatever is chosen by the person, it is used as a numbing agent of course. Anything that takes away the pain temporarily without having to work through the situation is enough to keep people in bondage for a long time. The problem with all numbing agents is that they don't deal with the real problems. Instead, they push them down only to explode someday like a dormant volcano. My problem was not that I turned to any substance, not at first; I'll get to that later. Instead, I used the self-coined phrase, "dishes don't wash themselves," to motivate me to keep going. Those four words would drive me into the mental state of a busybody, moving quickly and constantly, but never really getting anywhere. I was refusing to grieve. My days became an endless cycle of the same events. Every day I would wake up, go to work, come home, and put myself to work doing meaningless tasks to keep myself from thinking about the reality that was happening around me. "Dishes don't wash themselves" became my motto for everything I did. Staying busy was the only thing allowing me to lie to myself and to show others, "I'm fine."

Some people consider that a good thing. They think it means they are tough. From personal experience of being "that guy," I would say they are crazy. If that is where you are now, stop fooling yourself. It was not good that I neglected the feelings I had inside myself. Speaking those words over my life was like slowly poisoning myself until I was mentally and emotionally dead. My phrase, "dishes don't wash themselves," was really me saying, "I don't have time, or rather I don't want, to process my feelings." Like I said, that is not a good thing. Those feelings I tried so hard to suppress would one day explode like a bomb, not only hurting myself but all those around me.

Although staying busy worked for a while, eventually I was forced to face my feelings head on and actually allow myself to process. I believe that many people dealing with divorce are doing the same thing I did. You choose not to process because then you have to accept that things didn't work out. For some, you may have to accept that you made a mistake. Even worse you have to accept that your life was not the picture perfect Instagram filtered life you so often would pretend to have. Choosing to process is choosing to face the pain head on. It is choosing to grieve. Maybe that is you. Maybe you are that person using the numbing agents of this world to push the pain away. If so, my prayer for you is that you would have the courage to walk through the process of actually grieving. Begin to accept that it is okay to not be okay for a while. Just remember, it is not okay to stay there.

Am I Going Insane?

I know the word "insane" may seem a little extreme, but I can think of no other word to describe the emotions I was feeling. I was at a place in my life I had never been. If I wasn't completely insane then it was definitely the closest I would ever like to be to it again. The feelings of going insane are quite different than anything else I have felt. My mind was gone. I couldn't think straight. I felt like everybody was against me. Ultimately, I lost trust in everybody around me. Anybody and everybody that was in my circle or in my life was automatically pushed away. Due to me making sure my dishes were clean and that I kept busy, I ended up mentally isolating myself just as much as I was physically isolating myself. The scariest part is that I did it without even knowing it. It was the mental isolation that led me to keep everybody at an arm's distance. Just close enough to keep an eye on them but far enough away to keep them from hurting me.

Dishes Don't Wash Themselves

Looking back, it really does amaze me how in an instant life can change. One minute I am saying I am just fine and the next I cannot even think straight. This is the part of divorce people understand the least until they have been through it. We always see external factors such as a spouse moving out, kids having to be separated from parents, separation of finances, and separation of possessions. Sometimes, we even see things that can be perceived as good during this time. However, what we cannot see is the mind. That is where the real battle takes place. Yes, the courtroom is intimidating, but the mind is something you cannot escape from. At least a mediation hearing only lasts a half hour and you go home, but the thoughts in your head follow you there.

This was the moment of divorce I was not prepared for. Who knows how to prepare for a moment in life that you never expect to come? Like I said before, I don't know of any person that enters a marriage with the intention of divorcing in the future. That is why I believe when we are faced with divorce, we all have similar unhealthy processes of dealing with it. Not because we are some terrible people, which the devil would have us believe, but because we were not mentally, physically, emotionally, or spiritually prepared for the battle we just entered into. Therefore, many of us end up in this place with feelings of insanity. We don't know who to trust, or if there is anybody we can trust anymore. We end up isolating ourselves from the very people that want to help us.

Somebody reading this book is living in isolation. It may not even be physical isolation. Some of you are mentally isolating yourself by creating false narratives about those around you and the way they must think about you. You allow those narratives to grow like seeds planted in the garden of your mind until you see these people no other way. For others you are living in emotional isolation. You may find yourself surrounded by people all the time having to hide the fact that you are now in mental hell. You have cut off everybody emotionally and allowed your heart to become callose towards others love and affection all become of that one person that hurt you. You may be doing a great job hiding it right now, but you won't be able to keep up the charade forever. The truth will be brought to light. The good news is that you can let your guard down today. You can go back to that one friend, family member, pastor, leader, mentor, whomever it is and admit where you are. Start the process of healing today before you end up like I did and find yourself at rock bottom.

Hit Rock Bottom

The idea of hitting rock bottom has been used as a metaphor by many. As I look at my process of "grief," or lack thereof, rock bottom is the one metaphor fitting to describe the cold, dark place I found myself. I lost a lot during this season of my life. I was twenty-five years old when I lost my marriage, my ministry, and my mental health. Not to mention the truck I had to sell, the house I had to sell, and my life savings that had to be used. Due to my lack of ability to find a healthy coping mechanism in light of all I was dealing with, I found myself turning to the only thing I knew to turn to. I turned to my past. By doing so, I found myself back in a place of substance abuse with alcohol like never before. It was nothing for me to drink three full bottles of whiskey a week. I found myself waking up, only to take enough shots to fall back asleep. I had nobody to talk to, to hold me accountable, or to be open with. The finished product of self-inflicted pain caused by allowing myself to be isolated is now being manifested in a person I never wanted to be again. I had hit rock bottom, and I wasn't sure how I'd ever make it out.

Dishes Don't Wash Themselves

This is a scary place to be. For me, I knew my faith was firm in Jesus, but my reality was that life was spiraling out of control. So, I chose to comfort my reality rather than confront it. I decided to numb my pain instead of calling on Jesus to heal it. Many people going through divorce that have had a past with substance abuse can easily find themselves right back in a situation they never thought possible. Divorce does something so mentally and emotionally powerful to the human soul that it would make even the holiest of men and women stumble and fall. My fear is that some of you are in this place and like me, you don't want help. You want to stay where you are and just drown your sorrows in whatever your numbing agent is. For some it is substance, others it may be social media, television, food, shopping, self-loathing, self-inflicted pain, suicidal thoughts, anger, rage, whatever it is you use to numb the real feelings you have. The feelings that you are not worthy and that you have messed up beyond what God can fix. Let me say this, that is a lie. If you are still breathing, God is not done with you!

If you are at rock bottom, get help today. My first step in healing was asking for help. You will never receive the help you don't ask for. Yet you have to humble yourself and realize you are not the first person going through a divorce that has dealt with what you are dealing with. There is help for you, but you cannot stay quiet. I can assure you, rock bottom is no place to live. If you stay too long, you may not come out alive.

Regained Trust

Oftentimes when people face a situation like divorce, they lose trust in a lot of people. They start viewing lifetime friendships as enemies with a hidden agenda, family members as judgmental towards you, and co-workers as "snarky know-it-alls" telling you what to do next. It will make you even more mad that those "snarky know-it-alls" telling you want to do haven't even been in your shoes. Much like myself, people in this stage begin to separate themselves, isolate themselves, and keep people at that impenetrable "arm's distance." I remember being at this stage for a long time. Even after my divorce was final, I still didn't let people into my life. In my opinion, I learned my lesson that I couldn't trust people. It didn't matter who they were, their job title, their social status, or all their promises to me. The bottom line was that all people are the same, and they can't be trusted.

The problem with this way of thinking was that while I was verbally claiming my distrust was towards people, I was internally proving my distrust was towards God. I lost sight of daily prayer. I found myself not wanting to be around God's people. My devotion time was sparse at best. Yet, I would try to surround myself with friends or family to get over my pain. I was trying to listen to everyone else and you know, "get out more." All that is good, but none of those things are the solution. The Bible is clear that, "God's ways are not our ways and His thoughts are not our thoughts" (Isaiah 55:8-9). So, when the world says get out to find peace, God says look in to find peace. Look into His Word. Look into His promises. Look into His love for you. By looking out I was proving that my trust problems were not in others, they were in God.

Heck, I was depending on others to get me out of the emotional funk of divorce. What that picture tells me is that my real issues were with God because had it not been, I would have been seeking Him over everything else in that stage of my life. I would have been spending more time in the Bible than in the bottle. More time in prayer than in perversions. More time with

God than with my own guilt. My actions proved, although I kept people at an arm's distance, I still depended on them over God to keep me sane. Meanwhile, I was keeping God at a heart's distance, which is far more dangerous.

Many of us don't want to admit it but when we have gone through something like divorce, our biggest trust issue is with God, not man. Think about it. There are parts of the divorce that you blame God for. If you are a wife and your husband cheated on you then you may blame God for allowing him to ruin your family. Maybe you are a husband who didn't know your wife was seeing another man. Sure, you blame on yourself for a while, but now you have shifted your blame towards God. How could God allow such things to happen to you or your kids? We all face this same temptation to blame God when things are bad. We are experts at crediting Him with all the bad, but not praising Him for all the good. However, it is important to learn now, you cannot blame God for everything. Sometimes we bring things on ourselves, and other times things just happen. However, it is not always God's doing. So, your first step in regaining trust in people is regaining trust in God. The truth is that we have to come to terms with the fact that what we are going through is not God's fault. Before we get to that point, we must first understand more about divorce itself.

CHAPTER TWO GROWTH PLAN

1. List any unhealthy mindset that you have adopted because of divorce. It could be anything from a mantra to a thought processes.

2. Being brutally honest with yourself, where are you in the stages of grief mentioned in this chapter? How long have you been in that stage?

3. How has divorce affected your trust in God?

4. List all of the areas in your life where you recognize that you are no longer trusting God.

5. Who can you trust to share what you are feeling right now? Write that person's name down. Find a time to speak with them. Don't wait until you hit rock bottom, or maybe you're already there. Either way, share with someone!

CHAPTER THREE:

THE "D" WORD

I once heard a story about a young college aged girl who was going to visit her grandparents for the weekend. It just so happens to be the weekend of her grandmother and grandfather's fiftieth wedding anniversary. First of all, they deserve a standing ovation. Fifty years is a long time to be representing God through the holy covenant of marriage. It is a testimony in itself to what I am sure was considerably hard work. If you have been married you know, it is work, hard work. I often say marriage is the toughest, yet most rewarding thing you could ever enter into. Anyway, when the young girl arrived on her grandparent's doorstep she was greeted with a great big hug and a smile. The young girl congratulated her grandmother on fifty years of marriage and said, "Wow, after fifty years I cannot believe you never once considered divorce." The grandmother looked back at her granddaughter and said, "Yep, divorce was never an option. I considered killing him a few times but never divorce."

As funny as that is, I believe this story tells a lot about how we view marriage in the church, and even more so, how we view divorce. Many people view the word divorce as a word that should never be mentioned in church. It should not even be in your vocabulary. It is almost a curse word. If you ever hear anybody use the word divorce in church it sends chills down your spine, especially if you are the senior pastor. As a matter of fact, the handful of times I have heard the word divorce used in the church it was usually preceded by, "God hates." Most pastors would rather hear that somebody in their congregation committed murder than got a divorce. Think about it. At least the church would not have to deal with the "repercussions." One person would be dead, and the other person would be in jail. We wouldn't have to make those "tough churchy decisions." You know, like, can they still be a member? Can they still serve on the outreach team? Can they still be a part of the worship team? Can they still share a testimony? Can they still be a deacon, elder, or bishop? Can they still preach? Can they still work in the kids' department? Can they still be an usher, greeter, or run the connection desk? How long is the "restoration process?"

I am not sure what titles your church uses, but you get the point. The only question we don't ask is can they still give to God's church through their monthly tithe? We don't ask that question because it is a resounding, YES! Of course, we want your money. Seriously, I know it sounds morbid, but murder would make it easier. I once heard Pastor Kris Valloton, Senior Associate Leader at Bethel Church in Redding California, say that divorced people are the "modern day lepers" of the church. What a profound, yet true, statement for many churches and church goers. There are two reasons I believe we treat divorced people as such.

Number one, we simply do not understand divorce. So, we default to the limited understanding that we do have. Many have grown up listening to pastor after pastor say the same thing over and over about divorce, and we take it and run with it. We all know what it is, "GOD HATES DIVORCE." So, once we meet somebody that has been divorced, we keep them at an arm's distance as if the disease will somehow jump off of them and into our lives or marriages. We don't associate ourselves with them because they are now somehow a bigger sinner than we are. I have even met people that believe since God hates divorce, He must hate the divorcees, and that is why they can't be used in church. However, that is completely false and against God's character. Now, I am not here to argue against the fact that the Bible does say that God hates divorce in Malachi 2:16. I just hope that you would take the time to study and understand that verse before you run around spewing it out all over the place every chance you get, mostly completely out of context. We will get to that later.

However, those that have never taken the time to study and understand the reason the Bible says that God hates divorce in Malachi will always hang tight to it and condemn those who go through it. All the while they neglect hundreds of other verses in the Bible that could bring life back to an individual or their situation. You know, those verses about grace that seem to apply to every situation except divorce. I mean we read a Bible that many of the books in it were written by murderers, but God cannot use a divorced person, right? Wrong! I was being sarcastic if you could not tell. The problem is that many people do not study or test what they think they know any longer because it would force them to possibly change what they always thought to be true. Oh, and I don't know if you have noticed but people don't like change, especially in the church.

That leads me to my second point. I believe a natural part of our world now is to push aside all those things that do not affect us directly. We have done this with divorce in the church. Those who have never been faced with a divorce or have never had a divorce directly affect them just ignore the topic altogether while maintaining very strong views on the topic. I believe it is the same way with anything else. You don't study drug addiction until one of your children or family members begin to struggle with it. You do not take time to look up cancer and its effects on the body until somebody in your life has been diagnosed with it. We stand firm on our beliefs on homosexuality until we find out our own family members or friends struggle with it.

Proximity brings about passion. We aren't passionate about a subject until it affects us. We do not take time to learn about biblical divorce until you go through or have somebody close to you go through a divorce. I am guilty just like everybody else. I never cared about divorce until it happened to me. Once you have to deal with a situation that directly affects you, it forces you to finally take the time to learn about it. Therefore, when I found myself face to face with what at one point was "not an option," it forced me to do a little more research on this "D" word. I mean if I planned on being a divorced preacher, I better be able to defend it.

Defining Divorce?

First things first. In order to begin "Divorcing Divorce," we need to understand the definitions of divorce. What better place to start than with Merriam-Webster's definitions of the word "divorce." The first definition we will look at is just the bare bone meaning of divorce.

1: the action or an instance of legally dissolving a marriage.

2: separation, severance.

There you have it. Merriam-Webster describes divorce in two different ways. We see that divorce is described in a legal format and then again in a more generic form of separation. Although I appreciate both definitions, my favorite ones are the ones we use when trying to describe divorce to the English learner. They are as followed:

1: to legally end your marriage with (your husband or wife).

2: to make or keep (something) separate.

I think you would agree, the English learner's definition is just easier. I know they both basically say the same thing, but the extra attention to detail makes it for better understanding. I especially love the second definition because it is the backbone of this entire book. Divorcing divorce literally means to separate yourself from the shame, guilt, false identity, feeling of failure, and anything else Satan tries to mark your mind with as an attempt to keep you from reaching your full potential in Christ. Once the legal definition of divorce is imprinted into your state records, not to mention your testimony, Satan loves to use it any chance he gets. It is almost like a big red stamp that reads, "DIVORCED," in big bold letters. He will stamp it anywhere he can.

On your next church visit when you fill out the connection card that asks about your relationship status. On your next trip to the hospital when they ask your marital status on the paperwork. In your next relationship when you have to explain why you have kids, or maybe why you are so insecure about dating again. Shoot, now some jobs even ask if you have ever been divorced on their applications. The even more difficult part about it, if you are in ministry, is that they almost immediately skip over your application like you are damaged goods simply by being honest and checking the divorced box. The point I am making is that the word divorce carries with it a lot of weight. Not to mention the added weight by the church, by friends, or even by yourself, on those who currently carry around the word like an added accessory to their already full wardrobe. Even worse, when the word "divorce" is coupled with words like unforgivable, unlovable, failure, etc. We are creating a recipe for disaster. If you choose to continue to carry that weight the rest of your life you will always view divorce as that big red stamp, and you will crumble every time Satan stamps it.

Making a Positive Out of a Negative

The one thing we cannot do is change the entire human language to eliminate the word that we all hate to hear. Whether you are single, married or divorced, we can all agree the word itself seems to carry a very negative connotation. For some, it takes you back to those moments of mom and dad tearing the family apart in your young minds when they decided to pursue a divorce in your childhood. You couldn't believe that mom would want to do such a thing, or that dad didn't care enough to fight. For others, it is those haunting memories of him coming home late, or maybe not at all, and then smelling the other woman's perfume on him when you finally do see him. Whether you have witnessed a divorce, been through a divorce, or neither, we can all agree that the word itself is hardly thought of as positive. I believe Satan wants to keep it that way for those of us that have been through a divorce. However, what if I told you, the very word that has been captivating your mind and taking over your emotions for years, can be used against itself for a positive outcome? What if we could take a word that carries so much negativity, and turn it into a positive for our situation by using its very definition against itself?

My mom will be very proud of me for this section of the book. She is a math genius. She loves mathematics so much that she used to carry math books to my football games my senior year of high school. That is not a joke! One thing that my mother would love to tell you about is the fact that in math you can make a positive out of two negatives. Anytime you multiply or divide a negative number by a negative number, you get a positive. Wow! That is pretty interesting. Well, not to most, but to my mother that is cooler than when we landed on the moon! Seriously though, what if we did the same thing with the two definitions we just learned about? What if we decided to take the two definitions that seem to be negative, multiply them by God's grace, divide them by God's power, and voila, divorce is now a positive word?

Let me be clear. I am not saying getting a divorce is positive. What I am saying is if we use the formula and begin *divorcing divorce*, we take the two definitions, and use them against each other. For example, try taking the second definition of divorce we learned about above and apply it before the first definition. You would literally be saying that you are separating yourself from the definition that tries to define you as no longer being with your husband or wife. Not to mention all the feelings that come along with that definition. Once we do that, we can begin to divorce those negative feelings about being divorced. We can begin to divorce those negative memories. We can begin to divorce those emotions that Satan uses to keep us in a place of bondage. You know, the fears about how nobody could ever want to be with me after knowing that I have been divorced.

Maybe it is the doubts that Satan puts in your head about how you will ever meet another woman or man that will accept the fact that you have kids from a previous marriage and love them as their own. It might even be the feelings of unworthiness or unwantedness you have deep in your inner soul. Satan is the father of lies. He has many of you believing the lie that you will always have to carry the weight of your divorce. Almost like it is something that you deserve because of your past mistakes. However, I believe that as you begin to separate yourself from those negative thoughts, negative feelings, feelings of unworthiness, or feelings of failure, then you will finally be able to divorce the divorce. You will finally live in the freedom of grace that God has called you into. In order to divorce or separate yourself from the things that hold you in bondage, you must first do your own little study. For some of you, this is going to challenge everything you have ever thought about divorce. However, the only way to experience freedom is to know the truth. The truth that is found in no other place, but the Bible itself.

CHAPTER THREE GROWTH PLAN

1. How does the word "divorce" make you feel?

2. Have you felt like others treat you differently because you are divorced? If yes, how so?

3. List all the lies you have been believing about your divorce.

4. What fears do you have with divorcing divorce?

5. What gives you hope about divorcing divorce?

CHAPTER FOUR:

WHAT DOES THE BIBLE REALLY SAY?

GOD HATES DIVORCE! We have all heard it. For many of you that one statement is all that plays through your mind when facing the harsh reality that divorce is on the horizon. It seems to plague your mental ability to think about God in any other way. The question then becomes if God hates divorce, how does He feel about me? If He hates divorce does He hate me because I am divorced? Even more so, am I somehow disqualified from ministry, serving, or having a leadership role in the Kingdom of God that I love so much? We have so many questions with so many different answers depending on who we talk to, how they were raised, and their denominational background. Trust me, I dealt with these same questions and even fears. It wasn't until I was going through divorce that I decided to study it. Like I said before, proximity brings about passion. Yet, what I found was quite interesting, not to mention, rarely taught! Not that I have not found some lost "divorce theology" that will somehow make divorce okay. That is not the case. I do not believe God ever wants marriage to end in divorce. What I have found though is how the church has misunderstood God and His reasons for hating divorce. Let's take a deeper look into the Bible to see what it really has to say about this terrible thing called divorce.

Dissecting Divorce

If you do enough research, you will find that the Bible doesn't mention divorce all that much. So, it is easy to understand how human influence and interpretation can begin to shape someone's understanding of the few scriptures we do have. Especially when they are as blunt as Malachi 2:16 (NLT) that states,

> 16 "For I hate divorce!" says the Lord, the God of Israel. "To divorce your wife is to overwhelm her with cruelty," says the Lord of Heaven's Armies. "So guard your heart; do not be unfaithful to your wife."

I mean, how do you argue against that? Well, the truth is… you can't. God does hate divorce. But just because He hates divorce, doesn't mean He hates you. We have to know why God hates divorce, and I can assure you it is probably not why you think. I bet you think it is because divorce is sin. Of course, that is what you think. God hates divorce because it is a sin. That is what you have been taught. But what if I told you that divorce is not always a sin? WHOA!!!! Somebody just got the urge to throw this book away. Some pastor is going to take this line and run with it for the rest of my career. "I don't like that pastor. He says divorce is okay." Well first of all, that is not what I said. I do not believe divorce is okay. Yet that doesn't mean I have to assume that in all cases divorce is a sin for everyone involved. In fact , I don't believe that. I believe that sin is always involved in divorce but not every divorcee is involved in sin. Just because God hates something doesn't mean it is sin either. Where do I get this proof, you ask? Let's connect the dots with a little discussion that carries a lot of weight with the church in Matthew 19:3-9 (NIV):

> 3 Some Pharisees came to him to test him. They asked, "Is it lawful for a man to divorce his wife for any and every reason?" 4 "Haven't you read," he replied, "that at the beginning the Creator 'made them male and female,' 5 and said, 'For this reason a man will leave his father and mother and be united to his wife, and the two will become one flesh'? 6 So they are no longer two, but one flesh. Therefore what God has joined together, let no one separate." 7 "Why then," they asked, "did Moses command that a man give his wife a certificate of divorce and send her away?" 8 Jesus replied, "Moses permitted you to divorce your wives because your hearts were hard. But it was not this way from the beginning. 9 I tell you that anyone who divorces his wife, except for sexual immorality, and marries another woman commits adultery."

You may be asking yourself, how is he going to weasel himself out of this scripture? I am not. I don't have to. If we read it and understand the full context, we will see clearly that divorce is not always a sin. How is that? Well, easy. Jesus permitted it under certain circumstances, and Jesus, being God, cannot sin. Nor would He permit others to sin. Yet, here we see plain as day that they were allowed to divorce their wives if they had been cheated on. Which honestly was highly unlikely being that it would be a sure death sentence. Now don't miss this next statement. While I believe that divorce in and of itself cannot be sin, sin is always involved in divorce. Whether it is one party or both parties. Someone had to have committed sin for a biblical divorce to take place. In order to grasp the context, we need to see what is really happening in this story.

First, we see that this is all a trap. They came to trick Jesus.

They were hoping to give Him a question that He couldn't answer. We have to see that this is a specific story between Jesus and a group of religious leaders asking about a specific type of divorce. They asked about a divorce known as "any cause" divorce. This was a type of divorce that allowed men to divorce their wives for any reason they felt necessary. These religious leaders were hoping Jesus would say "no you can't get divorced." I am sure they would have pointed Him to the Law of Moses at that point and deemed Him a false teacher. Instead, Jesus knowing their hearts, something He would reveal soon, went ahead, and asked them what was already on their hearts. He asked them to tell Him what Moses told them about divorce. They say that Moses said they could get divorced as long as they sent her away with a certificate.

Here is where Jesus smacks them in the face. Jesus states in this passage that Moses, through God, conceded to the hard sinful hearts of men by allowing them to divorce their wives for any reason. All they had to do was give her a certificate of divorce. God allowed that because of the evil heart of the men. This certificate was the one thing freeing her. Without it the woman was just put out on the street with no place to go. Think about the time period. A woman was essentially treated as a man's property. Prior to marriage, a woman would live at home under the protection of her father. Then she would be given to a man as a wife when she came of age to have children. In some cases, girls would be given in marriage in their early teenage years. When the marriage took place a dowry, or bride price, would be paid for the woman to her father. After being purchased by her husband she could no longer live in her father's house. So, in the days of Moses, we hear about a time that men would throw their wives to the curb without ever releasing her from the marriage. This put the woman in a bind because she was considered to be still married. That meant she could not go back to her father's house because she "had a husband" and could not be married to someone else because, yep you guessed it, she "still had a husband."

Therefore, the concession made in Moses's day was not so the men could run wild and divorce whomever they want. It was to protect the woman from ending up on the street as a prostitute because some man threw her out like a piece of trash for the next best thing. Jesus says, "That is not how it was in the beginning" meaning in the Garden. He is referring to when God gave Eve to Adam. God created Eve. God developed Eve. God spent time alone with Eve. God even presented her to Adam as a beautiful gift completing mankind with the masculine and feminine side of God. Showing the world that when they are placed together as a unit to do life with each other, they become the very representation of God on this Earth. So, when God gave Eve to Adam, He didn't expect Adam to give her back. The same was true with Israel when they were given a wife by the woman's earthy father. It was symbolic to God giving Eve to Adam (side note, God has a feminine side. Read Genesis 1:26-27).

That leads us back to Malachi 2. Why does God hate divorce? Because it tears the very fabric of God's heart. Marriage is what represents God on this side of heaven. When a husband and wife reconcile, we see God. When a husband and wife forgive each other, we see God. When a husband and wife show grace to each other, even when the other doesn't deserve it, we see God. Therefore, we see God hates divorce because it not only puts a stain on His name by those who claim to follow Jesus, but also because of the pain it causes His children. Not because it is some unforgivable sin. The truth is that nobody makes it through to the other side of divorce without irrefutable, and in some cases, irreparable damage. So, it is important for us to remember the whole truth of God, and His word, when it comes to wading through the emotional waters of divorce.

One truth is that just because you have been through a divorce doesn't mean you throw out the rest of the Bible all because of a few understudied or misunderstood interpretations of scripture. We need to remember the other scriptures we also know to be true. God may hate divorce, but He is madly in love with you. It is easy to begin losing sight of God's love and affection for us during the many moments we are lacking both physical love and affection from a spouse we once were ecstatic about. However, your situation may change, but God does not. The Bible is clear that God is the very essence of love (1 John 4:8). So, if God is love, He doesn't hate you because you are no longer married. He hurts for you, but He doesn't hate you. God always hurts for His children when they are hurting. Even if you are the reason for the divorce. Let's say you are reading this, and you know the sin that caused your divorce. Let's say it was your fault. You have to accept that God also loves you! He is willing to forgive you of that wrongdoing and restore you back to His love and affection.

The most important thing to remember when divorcing divorce is understanding what God really thinks about it. How and why He hates it. This frees us from the idea that we have some stain or blemish beyond repair. This frees us from the lie that we can't be used by God anymore. This frees us from the lies that we have heard so many times that because God hates divorce, He must hate me. Let me be very clear; I am not saying that God is okay with Christians getting divorced. That is not true. Remember, God does hate it because of the sin and pain that are always involved. However, in the same way God hates it, He doesn't hate you because of it. He is a loving and gracious

God. The issue is that we tend to lose that loving gracious voice of God amidst the chaos of the newfound challenges of our divorced lives. It is like that voice gets drowned out by another voice. One that is full of lies and deceit. One that holds no power, but the power we give it. That is the voice of our enemy, the devil.

CHAPTER FOUR GROWTH PLAN

1. How does the phrase, "God hates divorce" make you feel?

2. Now that you understand why God hates divorce, how does it make you feel about His continued love for you?

3. Since we know that God continues to love us, how does that help you to love yourself?

4. Who else do you know that needs to hear the truth about why God hates divorce?

5. What is holding you back from sharing it with them?

CHAPTER FIVE:

THE ENEMY

I know it sounds crazy, but my absolute favorite book of the Bible is Genesis. I love the book of Genesis because it gives us the very history of who we are, why we are here, and why we struggle the way we do. It is the basic platform for our first understanding of creation, sin, the fall of humanity, and so much more. Along with all of that, we are also introduced to a very real, very powerful, very evil, spiritual force. This particular force is in direct opposition to everything you are or meant to be. He goes by many names in the Bible but just to name a few, you may know him as Lucifer, Satan, or the devil. Lucifer is known to have once been a beautiful angelic being that once held a high place in the heavenly realm. That is until he rebelled against God and was cast out of heaven. Many people believe that the devil has been God's enemy ever since, but that's not true. The devil is not God's enemy. The devil is your enemy. The word "enemy" carries a connotation of a worthy adversary. However, God is so big and mighty there is no worthy adversary.

There is no one that can defeat Him or come close. So, we have to stop looking at the devil as God's enemy and see him for what he is, our enemy. He is after us. He has already lost to God through Jesus on the cross. There is nothing he can do to stop, distract, or defeat God, but there is a lot that he will do to you.

I often say, *in order to defeat your enemy, you must know your enemy*. The problem with the majority of Christians today is that we know of the devil, but we don't know him. I have found that most Christian churches avoid the conversation of the devil all together. As if by doing so we are giving him more power than he already has. We love to talk about Christ and His love and His mercy, but we neglect talking about our number one enemy to all of those things.

Yet, if we want to be able to defeat our enemy, we must know him, meaning, we must study him. Think about it. Whether it is a sports team about to compete or an army going to war, they do the same thing. They study their competition, or enemy, for lack of better terms. They don't just randomly go into battle or into a game without any knowledge of who they are competing against. That is a fast track to total defeat. And that is what we are seeing today in the Church when it comes to the devil. Our lack of study and knowledge of the enemy is the very reason many Christians live in constant defeat by him. So, what do we need to know about the devil in order to defend ourselves in the battle? Well, the truth is, someone could write an entire sequence of novels on who the devil is and his tactics. So, I want to focus on just a few adjectives that describe the character of our enemy. This will help us know just how to defend ourselves when he comes to attack.

The Father of Lies

THE DEVIL IS A LIAR. I know you have heard it a thousand times but let me say it again. THE DEVIL IS A LIAR. If you want to know what the devil's character is like, the Bible tells us. He is a liar, but not just a liar, he is the father of lies (John 8:44). Jesus, Himself, says that the devil has been a liar from the beginning. Referring to the time he convinced Adam and Eve to eat of the fruit from the tree of the Knowledge of Good and Evil. This iconic moment took place just after the serpent, aka the devil, lied to Eve and said that she and her husband Adam would not die if they ate the fruit and disobeyed God. What the devil did in that moment was convince two people that were created by God, walked with God, and spent time with God, that God was somehow lying to them.

Just a few moments with the devil diminished the time spent with God with just one lie. "You will not die." But they did. We know the story. They even went and hid from God in the garden. Almost as if they are still listening to the serpent after they realize something went terribly wrong. I can hear him now, "You better go run and hide. God is going to be so mad at you." And that's what they did. They ran and hid from God like children in fear of getting in trouble.

Does that sound familiar? It kind of sounds like us as Christians when we start believing the lies the devil is telling us. I mean we were created by God, walk with God, spend time with God, and yet sometimes the devil's lies sound so true. They feel so real. As if every negative word spoken over our life about who we are or who we are to become is inevitably true. At least that was the case for me. The devil had sold me a whole lot of lies that I bought up like cheap candy after a holiday sale. I mean anything he told me I clung to as if it was the voice that would lead me out of this wilderness where I found myself. Like when he told me that I was a failure because I was divorced. Or when he would say that I screwed up my life and my future in ministry. Or when he told me nobody would ever love me because I was now damaged goods.

I not only began believing the lies but also believing that everyone else was against me in the process. That's because the enemy's voice was the only voice I had chosen to listen to. As much as I wanted to hear from God, I was not in His word. I did not dive into the scriptures for healing the way I should have. Instead, I dove headfirst into a bottle of whiskey, more like several if I am honest. The next few years became a living nightmare of addiction and depression all because of the voice that I chose to listen to.

I am writing this today in hopes that you do not take the same path I took. If you don't choose to divorce divorce the healthy way, which is through God's word, His love, and His people, you will end up in a place you don't want to be. We see how our enemy's lies can play a pivotal role in shaping us if we are not careful. If he is the "father of lies," then that means there is no truth in him. Nothing he will say to you will ever lead you to a better place in this life. In fact, he actually likes to take the truth, twist it, and feed it back to you as a pretty packaged lie in disguise.

I have seen in my own life how this takes place, but also in the lives of others. For example, I have seen single moms going through divorce that believe nobody will ever want to be with them because they have children. They would even say things like, "Who wants to take care of someone else's children?" While their psyche and understanding seem to be valid, we see that they have left no room for God in that picture. Yes, they are divorced and yes, they have kids, but that doesn't mean that there isn't someone out there being prepared for them and their children. I have witnessed men who have lost it all due to their infidelity in the marriage. Then the devil comes in and begins to tell them how horrible of a person they are. He will have them convinced that nobody loves them. That even their kids will never forgive them. He tells them that they messed up so badly that they should just end their life.

Somebody reading this feels that way right now. You feel like you have caused way too much damage and that the best solution would be for you to no longer be alive. Once again, this is a lie from the devil. Just because damage has been done, doesn't mean it can't be dealt with. Notice I didn't say fixed. Sometimes damage is done beyond repair, and it can't be fixed. That is okay. Recognizing that you can't fix what was broken may be the first solution to moving forward. It might be exactly the truth you need to face in order to start moving on to a healthy life instead of trying to rebuild from rubble. The point I am making here is that the devil's number one weapon is to lie. He is a master at lying and convincing others of the lie. Just look back at the story I shared earlier of Adam and Eve. The enemy lied to Eve, convinced her of the lie, and even was able to use her to lie to Adam. This is what led to the original curse of sin that we are all under today. How did this start? With a lie? That is what the devil wants to do is to lie to you. He will say, "Drink this, and it will make you feel better. Eat more of this, and it will make you feel better. Go find someone to meet your sexual needs, and it will make you feel better."

But you will never hear him offer up a solution that actually causes you to lean more on God. In fact, every lie he feeds you will cause you to end up further from God and His truth. This is what separates the devil's voice from God's voice. Is what you are hearing leading you closer to God or further away? The lying voice of the devil will always lead you away from God. Just like when Adam and Eve ran and hid from God in the garden playing what would be the first ever game of hide and seek, all because of the lie they believed. While you can hide from God all you want, He is the greatest seeker to ever exist. He seeks not to punish you but to restore you! Look what He did to Adam and Eve. Yes, there were consequences to their actions, but God clothed them, covered them, and then commanded them to continue in the mission He had originally called them to, which was to rule and take dominion over the Earth. Although we may feel that we messed up God's call and plan for our life because of our divorce, we haven't. God is calling you to divorce that lie the devil has made you believe. He is calling you to divorce that identity you have adopted. He is calling you to divorce the divorce and cling back to the call He has always had on your life. However, you must remain vigilant. The devil is not just a liar. He is also a lion.

A Roaring Lion

How many of us have just been like, "Devil why?" Not "God why?" But "Devil why? Why are you still bothering me? Why are you still on my case? Can't you just leave me alone now? I've already lost my marriage, my kids, and so much more." For some of you, you are there. Well, let me give you some tough love that is much needed. He is still bothering you because he is out to devour you. Yep, I can't sugar coat it. The Bible is clear what his cause is. His cause is to absolutely devour you. We see Peter say, "Stay alert! Watch out for your great enemy, the devil. He prowls around like a roaring lion, looking for someone to devour" (1 Peter 5:8, NLT). That means the enemy is out waiting to attack. He wants to attack in a way that will completely destroy you. And not just some of you, but all of you. He cannot have your soul, so he wants your time, your mind, your family, your marriage, and even your life.

The Enemy

The truth is the scent of every Jesus follower is on the nostrils of the enemy waiting for them to fall asleep. Waiting for them to get lost in the business of life. Waiting for them to grow tired of their spouse. Waiting for them to grow annoyed with their situation. He lingers in the background until they get tired and let their guard down so that he can attack. If you want to know why the devil is still bothering you, it is because that is what he does. He is forever a nuisance with no power. Except that which we give him. However, there is good news in all of this! Everyone knows that the enemy only attacks what is valuable to the other side. In this case, you are so valuable to God the enemy can't help but to attack you. The even greater news is that you already have victory over him through Jesus Christ. There is nothing that he can do to take away the value and love bestowed on you by God through His Son.

I know you have heard it a thousand times, but you need to hear it now more than ever. No matter what happened in your marriage. No matter whose fault it was. No matter how the marriage ended. No matter what your family and friends say. No matter how you are treated. No matter what the "church" says. You are still valuable. You are still loved. God's feelings for you never changed. If anything, His heart is more broken than yours over the pain you are dealing with. I know it is hard to imagine but remember what the Bible says, "For I hate divorce!" says the Lord, the God of Israel. "To divorce your wife is to overwhelm her with cruelty," says the Lord of Heaven's Armies. "So, guard your heart; do not be unfaithful to your wife." (Malachi 2:16, NLT). Remember that God hates divorce because it tears the fabric of His heart. Not because He hates you. So, when you feel like you are being preyed on by a roaring lion. When you feel the devil lurking in the shadows. Don't be afraid. Be satisfied. Be satisfied that the enemy still finds you to be of enough value to God that he can't help but to attack you. The truth is, he is scared of you!

I remember when I was going through my divorce. It seemed that I had a lot of people against me. I often felt like I was going toe to toe with the devil himself through some of the persecution I received. However, as I began divorcing divorce, I found it to be of great joy to be in the "ring" with the devil. It began to be an honor that God would consider me worthy of such a trial. Even more, that God would trust me to have the faith to endure it. I began seeing the opposition as an opportunity to grow in Christ. I had truly begun to live as James tells all believers when he said, "Dear brothers and sisters, when troubles of any kind come your way, consider it an opportunity for great joy. For you know that when your faith is tested, your endurance has a chance to grow. So let it grow, for when your endurance is fully developed, you will be perfect and complete, needing nothing" (James 1:2-4, NLT).

I love how he doesn't isolate which troubles we should consider as opportunities for great joy. He just says, "troubles of any kind." That means whatever troubles you are facing right now. It could be a vicious custody battle that you never thought you'd be dragging your children through. Maybe it is the plaguing emotions of utter loneliness, and the thoughts of never being loved again. It might be the addiction that has found its way into your life that you have adopted as your way of "coping." No matter the troubles James says to consider it joy. Why? Because it is an opportunity for God to make you stronger, build your faith, and at the end of it all, bring glory to Himself through what He did in your life.

The Enemy

I can tell you first hand that when you begin to live out the joys of being in persecution with your eyes and heart fully focused on Jesus, it will not only change your life, but those around you. When others see you smile, not through the pain, but amidst it. Fully recognizing you are hurting yet God is good. God is faithful! That draws others towards Him. It reminds me of the time when one of my former youth students approached me to tell me she had given her life to Jesus and wanted me to be the one to Baptize her. I was moved by her wanting me to be the one to conduct the Baptism, but what moved me even more was what led her to solidify her faith in Christ. She told me that she had been watching me. Kind of freaky at first, I know. But what an eye-opening truth for any Christian facing troubles of any kind, as James would say.

The truth is that the world is watching you! They are watching how you respond. They are watching to see if you are still desperately clinging to that "Jesus" guy, like you claimed to have when life was good. In the same way, this girl said she had been watching me over the last year. She saw all that I had gone through. She heard all the lies that were spread. She saw all I had lost. But she also said that she saw how my faith in Jesus never waivered. Did you catch that? All because I began to divorce divorce for my own sanity. All because I began to lean into Jesus and not run from Him when the enemy was attacking. All because I began to see the great joys in my trials, and my value to God. All because I decided to trust in what Jesus did for me on the cross, and the forgiveness He had given me. This young person saw His faithfulness and His strength in my life and knew then that He was real. What I heard her saying was, your hell was my help!

Wow! Have you ever considered that maybe, just maybe, what

you are experiencing with all of the devil's attacks are actually bigger than you? Don't get me wrong, I never set out to divorce divorce for anybody else but me. I wish I could say I walked by faith so that others would see Jesus. Honestly, I couldn't walk at all. Jesus carried me the whole way once I finally gave in. But I gave in to Him for my sake, nobody else's. Yet, God is a big God. So, He didn't just let me go through hardships, He decided to use them to heal someone's heart. I don't know about you, but if divorcing divorce leads to healing and in the process someone else finds Jesus, then it was all worth it for me! I don't want to make myself sound too good.

Remember, I didn't divorce divorce for that reason, but that is something amazing that came out of it. The truth is, I wish I had the guts to tell that teenage girl that my faith did waiver in the process. Many times. Sometimes, I think I might have even lost faith. But His love for me never left. That is what got me through. That is where my joy came from. That is how I was able to smile amidst the pain. Knowing that God didn't hate me, that He did still loves me, and that He was broken for me is what got me through. It allowed me to call out the lies of the devil and stand firm in the face of fear when I heard him prowling around making noise. Because that is all it was, noise. When you recognize the devil for who he is, a weak and defeated enemy that is only strengthened by the power we give him, it helps to stop giving him that power. When you do that, you'll see him as a roaring lion with no teeth. Just a lion in disguise if you ask me.

Angel of Light

I always find the image of the devil being a big red scary guy with horns and a pitchfork rather funny. Especially in light of how the Bible describes him. The Bible actually teaches that the devil is, how should I say, a little less "noticeable." I mean think about it. If the devil showed up every time as a red scary guy with horns and a pitchfork, I just don't believe we would be so easily manipulated by him. That is why it is important for us to know how the Bible describes him, as an evil being that masquerades as an Angel of Light (2 Corinthians 11:14). This is important to note: the Bible never refers to the devil as "The Angel of Light" or as "An Angel of Light". In fact, it's quite the opposite. Paul mentions in 2 Corinthians that Satan masquerades as an Angel of Light. That word "as" is huge! This means that he is a master pretender, but it's just a facade. No matter what he has to offer, it is never what he promises. He shows up in our lives through the many avenues that appeal to our sinful nature with more promises of health and prosperity apart from Jesus, only to leave us more empty than we were before. This is his course of action when it comes to taking down believers. Especially, vulnerable believers that are experiencing the hurts and pains of divorce.

One thing we know from the word of God is that the devil isn't dumb. I mean, in one sense he is pretty dumb for rebelling against his creator only to be thrown into a pit of fire at the end of his being, but besides that, the Bible calls him cunning. Let me say it like this, the devil knows what he is doing. He knows how to tempt people and make them fall. The truth is, he knows people's weaknesses. Like a lion lurking in the shadows, the devil studies his prey. He doesn't just wait for an opportune time to attack. No, he works to create an opportune time for an attack. He will show up in your life in a way that he knows can lead you towards sin and death. The devil is patient. His attacks may be swift when they come but that doesn't mean he wasn't patient in his planning. He knows our weaknesses. Planning and patience are simple tactics he uses to exploit our weakness when we are most vulnerable. It could be that you have a weakness of loneliness, so he shows up in the form of someone that allows you to feel that void. Like a drug you spend every second of every day with them numbing all the pain of the divorce you are experiencing or have experienced. Of course, that is only until the drug that you used to fill the void of loneliness is no longer satisfying. He may show up in the form of a substance. It could be as innocent as a glass of wine to take the edge off. You may or may not have ever been a "drinker" but for some reason it hits differently this time. The fact that for a short moment you were able to relax and just disconnect is a high in and of itself. What was once a seldom or social occurrence is slowly becoming a more habitual action. It's found its way into your daily schedule labeled, "night cap." That is justifiable, right? Wrong! The devil is just creating a course to reach a weakness that you may or may not know you have.

Trust me when I say that he will mask himself in any coping mechanism in order to keep you held in bondage. These are only a few things that the devil uses for divorcees. I recognize there are so many more ways he is trying to get to you. But do you recognize them? Is he bringing bad company in your life that you typically wouldn't hang out with, but in this season, you just want to cut loose? Is he cultivating an environment of pessimism around you that is causing you to lose hope in God's faithfulness? Is he using others' success to create resentment toward God in your life?

However, the devil masquerades himself in your life, knowing your weaknesses and where you are most vulnerable will help to defend against his attacks. Knowing where he wants to attack will help you prepare and build that area in your life. The truth is that nobody is above the attacks of the devil. Nobody is perfect in their discernment. Nobody makes all the right decisions all the time. The good news is that even when we fall, we don't fail God. As much as we already feel we failed so many others because of our divorce, we don't need to fall into the lie that we somehow fail God too. The lie that we let Him down and now He might be going to abandon us like many people may have done. The good news is that we can't fail God. He needs nothing from us to which His dependence is on our success or failure. That means that He still loves us. He can still redeem us. He still has a purpose for us. Even when we fall into the traps or lies of the devil. Understanding God's love for you, despite you, is what will break the strongholds of the enemy in your life.

God is Still in Control

This is the harrowing question God asked the devil in the opening chapter of the book of Job in the Bible, "Have you considered my servant Job?" Just before, the devil is asked by God where he had been. As if God didn't already know. I see this as God showboating His Omniscience, all knowing power, almost as if He is reminding the devil of his place in the heavenly realm. Job is believed to be the oldest book in the Bible. Pre-dating Moses's writings. Many scholars believed that Job lived around the time of Abraham. His daily life consisted of worshiping God which included making sacrifices on behalf of his children who "may have sinned." Talk about a righteous man. He is making sacrifices just in case his kids did something wrong. The Bible also mentions that he was very wealthy and obviously blessed by God.

So, Job was known to give thanks to God through sacrifices for His blessings. Needless to say, he was devout. Then one day Job is blindsided by a series of events that would change his life forever and put his name and story into the greatest history book of all time, The Bible. All from that question, "Have you considered my servant Job?" Now I ask you, could you imagine your name being at the end of the question? For some of us that's exactly how we feel. We feel like Job's name has been replaced with our own. As though we have been offered up by God to the devil on a silver platter for him to devour us. We are questioning, "God WHY ME?" If you are there, you are not alone. Some of the greatest heroes of the faith have faced down those same feelings. They uttered those same words in their deepest times of distress. God why me?

If this is where you find yourself, there is good news. Just like Job, if you find yourself in the crosshairs of the devil, you can rest in this truth. God is still in control! He is aware of what is going on. Not only does He know what is going on, but He is not shocked either. God is not in heaven scrambling for a plan to figure out how to get you out of the mess you may feel you are in. He is the plan for your mess. He wants to turn your mess into a message about Him. So, it should give you peace that God is not surprised by your circumstances. In fact, He is in control of them. You may not understand what you are going through, but God always has a plan. This is just a test in which He will turn into a testimony if you keep your faith in Him.

When you begin to run toward God with all of the pains in your heart, and rest in the truth that He has not left you or abandoned you, then you will begin to experience the peace that surpasses all understanding like that Apostle Paul mentions in Philippians 4:7 (NIV). You will be able to resist the devil and he will flee from you, just as James wrote in James 4:7 (NIV). Resting in the truth that God is still in control is a reminder that God still has a plan for you. It restores the hope that God is not done with you. It replenishes your heart with God's love for you. Allowing yourself to rest in the comfort of God's control disarms the enemy completely because it shows him that you realize you already have the victory in Christ. There is nothing the devil can do to take that away. He can attack all he wants, but God wins and that means, you win!

I don't know where you are today, but I would be willing to bet it is not where you want to be. I don't know what lies you have already begun to believe or what road they have led you down. I don't know the attacks that the devil has brought upon you. I don't know the pain you have experienced. But I am sure of this, it is probably not where you want to be. If it were, you most likely wouldn't be reading this book. The good news is that wherever you are, you don't have to be there. Whatever path you are on, you don't have to keep walking it. Whatever damage you are continuing to create because of the lies you believe can stop. You don't have to continue to feed on the lies of the devil. What you are hearing now is not what you have to listen to. The coping mechanisms you've adopted don't have to continue. But the question is how? If I have been sold a lie by the devil. How can I return it? How can I trash it? Well, it goes beyond the lies themselves, and it takes us having a firm understanding of our identity. Not our identity in this world, but our identity in Christ.

CHAPTER FIVE GROW PLAN

1. In what areas of your life do you recognize the devil's temptations?

2. Write down all the lies you have begun to believe about your life, your children, your future, etc.

3. How can you begin to tell the difference between a lie from the devil, and the truth of God?

4. What has God revealed to you that you can do to make sure that you don't fall captive to the same lies again?

5. How can you guard yourself from falling into these temptations?

6. Write down one or two trusted Christian friends that you can open up to about the lies you have begun to believe. Then schedule a time to speak with them to help wade through the lies and find the truth.

CHAPTER SIX:

IDENTITY CRISIS

We see the commercials all the time, "watch out for those that want to steal your identity." Then they tell you to sign up for all of these identity theft plans regarding your social security number, bank accounts, driver's license, etc. You name it and they have a coverage plan for it. Yet, for most of us, we completely ignore all of those commercials because we have never had our identity stolen. Besides that one random charge across the country that our bank notifies us about and then declines it. Other than that, identity theft is far from our daily thoughts. I think that is why I had my guard down the day my identity was almost stolen. It was based on my own stupidity of course, but I will never forget how it transpired. You are probably going to think, "You're an idiot. You should know better," and I would say you are correct.

It was Wednesday morning. I was helping set up for a Bible club that a few guys at our church started in the middle school where our church services were held on Sundays. I was in such a hurry, rushing back and forth to our storage room, setting up lights, and putting chairs out that all I was focused on was the Bible club. In the meantime, I kept ignoring a phone call from a city in New Mexico. Normally, I would assume it was a scam and ignore the call, as I did, however, they kept calling. I began to think something could be wrong. So, when they called back the fourth time, I separated myself from everyone to see why whoever was calling needed my attention so badly. When I answered the phone there was a woman on the other line with an Islander accent. If I were to guess she was probably from the Bahamas. Upon my answer, she immediately said, "Mr. Gibson, I am calling you from the police department of such and such city in New Mexico to let you know that there is a warrant out for your arrest, and the U.S. Marshals are looking for you."

I am not going to lie, with my past with drugs I got a little scared. Then I reminded myself that it couldn't be true. Not only had I never been to New Mexico, but I wasn't a drug trafficker. So, I explained there must be a mistake. Yet, her urgency had me concerned. Again, she repeated my name, told me my address, and then reassured me the U.S. Marshals were looking for me. She told me that my next steps would be to turn myself in to the local police. I went into panic mode. I was thinking this can't be happening. I was rushing through old memories like flipping through a filing cabinet in my brain. What could I have done? Mind you, my past is not perfect, and I had old associates that could have very well used my name and been involved in drugs. So, the claim was not as far-fetched as it would be for some, but trafficking, and in New Mexico? No way! As I proceeded to tell the "police woman" that this couldn't be true she continued to state more facts about my life and asked more questions that had me even more confused and concerned. *Maybe somebody had stolen my identity?* I thought. I mean this lady really seemed to know just enough about me that she gained my trust. That is when it happened. She asked the question. Can you please confirm your social security number to make sure it is not another John Michael Gibson? I know what you are thinking, *you didn't*. Well...I did. I gave my full social security number, and as soon as I finished the phone hung up. It happened so fast

I assumed we got disconnected. I called back only to realize the number didn't exist. That is when it hit me, I had just had my identity stolen. I was tricked and deceived to the point I gave the one thing the person on the other end of the line needed to have access to my entire life. To think, I just gave it away.

As I reflect on that moment it reminds me of how easily we give up our identity in Christ during times of what we perceive as crises. It is not that we somehow lose our identities, it is that they are stolen from us through lies and deceit from the enemy. Just like the woman that called me knew just enough about me and my past to get me to fall for her lies. The enemy will do the same thing to all of us. We see the same thing with Eve, and the serpent in Genesis 3. The serpent deceived Eve by creating confusion in her mind when he asked, "Did God really say you must not eat from any tree in the Garden?" He immediately challenges God's word which causes her to see the possibilities in his claims. Satan still does that today. He whispers lies into the ears of all of us until we begin to believe them. Only to completely give up our identities because we chose to believe false information. The truth is this happens to all of us at some point in our lives when we deal with a crisis, but especially when dealing with divorce. In those moments it is easier for our flesh to desire the words of anybody but God because what God has to say just doesn't seem to be true at the moment.

It is much easier as a divorcee to side with the voices that say nobody will ever love you than to hear God say that He still loves you. It is easier to believe that you could never be forgiven for what you have done and that you deserve this pain than it is to believe that God awaits to forgive you. It is easier to accept that you are somehow tainted or used goods than to allow yourself to hope that God has more for you. The point is that Satan is a master when it comes to convincing you of things that just are not true. The Bible says that he was cunning in the garden when he deceived Eve. That means he is not an idiot. The lies he told Eve were believable just like the lies he tells you when going through something as difficult as divorce.

Like when he tells you that you will never find happiness again. Or that nobody will ever want to be with you because you carry the "baggage" of kids. Or that nobody wants to be with someone divorced because you must have done something to deserve it. Whatever the lie may be it is okay to be honest, at that moment you don't believe it to be too far from the truth. All Satan has to do is affirm them in your mind so that you will adopt them in your heart. Once you adopt the lie as truth, that is when you find yourself losing your true identity in Christ. Not just losing it as if it were a driver's license misplaced only to be found hours later. No, that is when your identity, the "who" that is inside of you, that person God made you to be, is stolen from you by the one person that wants nothing more than to destroy you.

While in the midst of my divorce I can honestly say I completely lost my identity. Not just for days or months but for years. When I tell you that regaining your identity is not an overnight thing please understand, I don't say that to discourage you but rather to encourage you. So that when you find yourself still trying to reclaim that person in Christ you are called to be months, even years down the road, you can remember that it is a process. It is not going to happen overnight, and God doesn't want it to. There is beauty in the process of finding who you are in Christ again because I assure you that it will not be the same person stolen from Christ. It will be someone completely new. Someone that is stronger. Someone that you don't even recognize. I believe that it is so hard for many of us to reclaim our identity in Christ. We spend so much time trying to get back to the old you before the divorce, but God wants to bring about a new you through the divorce. In order to do that, there is one, what I consider, "harsh realities," you have to accept in order to begin the process of reclaiming your identity in Christ. As hard as it will be to accept, it is a must in the process of divorcing divorce. Sorry for the face slap!

The Harsh Reality

I cannot lie. This section is one that hit me the hardest, not only writing it, but still living out these truths as I continue to grow and understand my identity in Christ. The first, and most difficult, harsh reality I came to accept was that the reason my identity was so easily stolen was because it was not matured. It didn't matter how long I had been a Christian, how many mission trips I had been on, how many churches I worked for, or how many sermons I had preached. The truth that was revealed during my divorce was that I was immature in my identity in Christ. Now, do not get this confused with being immature in my walk. There are differences. First of all, being immature in your walk with Christ is much more noticeable than being immature in your identity in Christ. Those that are immature in their walk tend to fall into more blatant sins and often find themselves in constant noticeable sin cycles.

Secondly, they also tend to fall among the categories of "new believers" or "stagnant Christians" if you will. While those who are immature in their identity in Christ not only hide it well, but they can also do so for years, be active in the faith, and not even be aware of their immaturity in their identity. It's just like the warnings and commercials to watch out for identity theft.

Identity Crisis

People ignore the fact that their identity is something that needs to be protected. The calls for protection go ignored because people don't really think it is something that will ever be stolen, especially when they are in Christ. Once accepting Christ into their lives many people fall into the temptation of working so hard to rid themselves of all sins and be disciplined in every area of their life that they neglect their identity in Christ, not realizing it is under that same attack by the enemy. The weight that your identity in Christ carries in relation to your Salvation and freedom from sin and death often goes misunderstood. We can become experts at not committing "big" sins, going to church, quoting the Bible, and serving others yet still not understand our identity in Christ. Therefore, we do nothing to mature it because we don't understand that it needs maturing, or because we assume that once we are saved our identity automatically comes to full maturity. Both paths of neglect will leave you in disarray and chaos about who you thought you were when divorce hits home. That is why many of you feel the way you do now.

So, how do we know if we are immature in our identity in Christ? Well, simply put, if you have never focused on your identity in Christ and the protection of it, chances are you need some maturing in that area. Let's look at a few identifiers that may reveal a lack of maturity in your identity in Christ. Take time to reflect on each of these to see if you can relate:

1. Blaming God for the hurt taking place in your life and forgetting that you are a child of His whom He would never choose to harm. (Romans 8:16)

2. Turning your back on God because you refuse to see how He could ever use something like a divorce to bring about His glory through His children. (Romans 8:28)

3. Refusing Godly counsel because you are tired of hearing Christian jargon in this time of pain forgetting that it is the words of your Father that will bring you the most peace. (John 16:33)

4. Going back to old, bad habits and sins, or even entertaining and indulging in new ones, while trying to fill the void that you lost and not going to your Father for comfort. (Matthew 11:28)

5. Resisting loneliness at all costs because of the emptiness you feel not realizing or accepting that you are never lonely with God. (Matthew 28:20)

You are forgetting who you are, and the Father that you have access to by not recognizing these areas in your life. Not to mention you are neglecting the power that you have access to that allows you to overcome this crisis. However, we can't stop with just recognizing we have a problem. We have to take steps towards allowing ourselves to live in freedom.

Getting It Back

The day I gave my social security number to the person on the other end of that phone started a whirlwind of emotions. My day went from normal to crazy in an instance. My mind was racing. I had to go to the police station, which was embarrassing. I had to start calling credit companies, banks, etc. Then to top it off I had to call my wife, which was more embarrassing! Yet, it was crazy all the hoops I had to jump through to work on getting it back and stopping more damage from being done in the future. I remember how quickly I felt the need to respond and how quickly I did. Then once I did all I could do, I had to wait. Now that is when it got weird. That is when the questions, worry, doubt, fears, all the emotions you can think of really began to take over. See, when I gave my identity away that was easy to recognize and easy to find the solutions to fix the problem. What I failed to realize is that after I did all I could do, there was still a process on the other end. The creditors had to do their job by putting my credit on hold. The banks had to do their job by canceling my cards. The police had to do their job by reminding me of how stupid I was for giving it away in the first place. It took several weeks for me to get my identity back, to get new bank cards and to unfreeze my accounts. It didn't just happen when I went and put the work in one time. There was an element of trust and patience needed. Trusting that those I called on for help knew what they were doing and that it would stop any further damage. Then patience to see if the work I did, along with trusting what they did, actually worked!

The point I am making is that the same is true for us when we are working to get back our identity in Christ. Recognizing we have an identity crisis isn't half the battle, it is a third of it. Then you have to start working through your maturity in Christ. You have to really take an introspective look at yourself and accept what areas of immaturity are in your life. Then begin working to mature in those areas. That is another third of the battle. The last third, is being patient with the process. You have to trust God to put a stop to the damage by doing what only He can do. So, when putting forth that effort to get your identity back you have to practice patience. Understand that things won't happen overnight. This is a process that takes time. Paul says it best in Galatians 6:9, NIV, "Let us not become weary in doing good, for at the proper time we will reap a harvest if we do not give up." If you continue to lean into God, He will come through on His end. The question is will you stay faithful on your end?

CHAPTER SIX: GROWTH PLANE

1. What part of your identity do you feel was stolen from you?

2. Do you find yourself wanting any pieces of the old you back? If so, what and why?

3. How can you change your thought patterns to believe that maybe God doesn't want to bring back the old you, but bring out a new you? What are some things you can implement?

4. What immaturity(s) do you feel you are currently struggling with? What can you do to begin maturing those areas of your life?

5. Having solid Christian people you trust to walk with you in life is critical. Who can you ask to walk with you as you work through these immaturities? Think of someone that will recognize when you are allowing them to dominate your focus and point you back to truth. (A church leader, trusted friend, family member, co-worker, etc)

CHAPTER SEVEN:

A NEW NORMAL

It quickly became a day I would never forget. For some, it was a day of confusion and chaos, but at the same time, for many others around the country and the world, it was a day of absolute stillness. A day of fear. A day of wonder. A day where everyone knew that we would be entering into a new normal. I was sitting in my 5th grade classroom just like any ordinary school day. I was most likely cutting up with friends or causing the teacher a headache. Let's just say "most" of my teachers liked me growing up, but I admit I could be a handful. However, on this day all shenanigans were quickly diminished by a quickly shifting atmosphere. Like when the clouds swiftly cover the sky making the bright light of the sun go dim. It all happened so quickly.

No one was prepared for the news we were about to receive, and the aftermath that would follow. The principal of the school came over the intercom and said something like, "Good morning, everyone, I want to make you aware that there is news coming out of New York City that an airplane has just hit one of the World Trade Centers." It was a moment that even as a young ten-year-old kid I knew something serious was going on. There is nothing like being a child staring in the face of an adult only to see that they seem more afraid than you are. Of course, all the fuzzy, box TVs hanging in the corner of every classroom were being turned on to watch the live media coverage. That is when we all witnessed the unthinkable. While still trying to comprehend the first plane crash, what was believed to be an accident at the time, we witnessed another plane hit the second tower of the World Trade Centers.

Now, I had no idea what the World Trade Centers were or how they had anything to do with me and my small town in South Carolina. I had never even heard of them at my age. I couldn't comprehend why all of a sudden, my little league football game was canceled, why kids were being pulled out of school, or why teachers were in tears? It didn't really make sense at the time how much September 11th, 2001 would change my life forever. Not just my life but everyone's life. Immediately, airport security beefed up, people were enlisting in the military all over the country to go to war, homeland security budgets more than tripled, and so much more. While terrorism was real, it became even more real by it reaching our borders so easily. Especially on a level of such high magnitude never before witnessed. So of course, it brought about change in how things were done and created a new normal for society in order to increase protection so that something like that would never happen again. The fact is things changed because things changed. Think about that. Go read it again.

We should always recognize in life that when things change, other things must change as well. I would often say, if something drastic changes in our church and things don't change, those following me as a leader should be terrified. That just means that I have fallen more stubborn than I already am and can't see past my own pride to recognize things might not be okay the way they used to be. The fact is that when things change in life, other changes are necessary. The day when four planes were hijacked with plans to attack on American soil and thousands of lives were taken, things changed. Because things changed, things had to change in other areas. For example, the transportation safety administration was implemented just a couple of months after the attack, better known as the TSA.

One of the biggest problems we have as humans is that we don't like change. We don't like the added time it takes to get through airport security, not realizing the safety measures they are taking to protect us. We don't like paying more in taxes to fund military efforts to stop terrorism in our country, not realizing that these things are necessary to keep us safe. I am not trying to be political or argue for or against war. What I am saying is that when things change around us, change in us is necessary. The problem most of us encounter is not that we don't recognize that we need to change, but it is accepting the new normal that comes with change. We know it is necessary even though we fight it so much. Why do we fight it? Because allowing change in our lives means being okay with letting go of things that maybe you thought you would always have.

It may mean allowing God to challenge everything you once believed about Him. It may mean completely deconstructing and reconstructing your life, habits, thought processes, etc. Either way it can be terrifying. Normal is comfortable. A new normal is challenging. There are a couple of things that I want you to learn from this chapter. They are biblical truths that when applied will allow you to experience the freedom that a new normal can bring. These are things I had to finally put into practice in order to reclaim my identity in Christ while divorcing divorce.

A New Normal

Learning to Trust

First thing is first, we have to learn to stop worrying. Trust me, I know what you are thinking. *Wow, so profound.* Yes, let me just all of a sudden stop worrying. Especially when worry, doubt, and fear are ingrained in our human nature as fallen creatures. So, why would I suggest something so impossible? If learning not to worry were so easy as typing it on a page why don't we just stop? I'll tell you why. We are so used to worrying that we often don't realize there is an alternative, which is to trust. We just assume because we worry we will always worry, so we let it dominate us. We don't even consider allowing our minds to shift into a new space of trust. Not just any trust but trust in God, the only one you can trust. The issue is that trusting in God requires believing in what you can't see while trying to look beyond what you can.

When going through a divorce worry is at the top of the list of mental problems. We are worried about finances, jobs, kids, and the future. Questions arise like where will I live? How will I afford the house? Do my kids hate me? Will my kids hate me? What will my family think? How are my friends going to react? Am I going to be able to make it on my own? So many emotions plague our everyday existence to the point we do just that, exist. We no longer live, we exist. We exist in our jobs, in our families, in our relationships, but in reality, because of the worry we experience we don't truly live. So how do we begin this worriless journey? Well, it begins with what I said before, by learning to trust God.

In fact, learning not to worry is not something to learn at all. Learning to trust in God is where you should be focused. By learning to trust in Him more you will notice your worry of worldly things will begin to dissipate. If you focus on learning not to worry all the time, your mind will only be focused on the worry. Then you will find yourself worrying about learning not to worry. Instead of going down that endless cycle, try applying your time to learning to trust God instead. I need to pause here. Notice I keep using the word "learn" or "learning." That is because what I am suggesting is a process. It is not something that takes place overnight. It's like learning math. In order to go further in mathematics, it starts with learning the basics of adding and subtracting. The same goes with trusting God. In order to go further with Him it starts with the basics. The basics are what make up the strong foundation. So, learning to trust God begins with allowing Him back in control of your tomorrow while you simply focus on today.

Jesus says in Matthew 6:33, NIV, "Therefore do not worry about tomorrow, for tomorrow will worry about itself. Each day has enough trouble of its own." Jesus is making a profound statement that we often quote but don't really live by, especially in times of trials. It is easy to say, "God, I trust you" all while holding on to your tomorrow, piecing it together to make it just right for you to control it while "giving God the glory." That is not trusting God at all. It is creating an illusion of trust on the outside while creating instability on the inside. Jesus tells us in Matthew 6 that God is in control of everything. That even the birds have food and the flowers are clothed in beauty. If God is taking care of the birds and the flowers how much more will He take care of us? Jesus is even recorded asking in Matthew 6:27 NIV, "Can any one of you by worrying add a single hour to your life?"

Yet, we learn from science, which does not oppose scripture, that worrying can actually decrease our life span. So, Jesus tells us that worrying does not help, and we see in the world that it actually hurts. So, why spend your life constantly worrying about the what ifs that are not even promised to come to pass? Why not spend your time trusting in the promises of God that are still for you despite the divorce you have gone through? Where did the hope go that God can turn everything into good for those called according to his purposes? Where did the belief go that God's grace is sufficient for you? Where did the awe go that God's love covers a multitude of sins? Where did you forget the truth that God is for you and not against you? Life is too short to live in worry about things outside of your control. So, stop wishing, wanting, and waiting on the old. It is time to accept that things have changed, therefore things must change. Learn to trust God again by letting Him have back what is rightfully His, your life.

Forgetting Forward

The second aspect of being freed by living in a new normal is putting into practice the words of the Apostle Paul, arguably one of the greatest missionaries to ever live, when he said in Philippians 3:13 NLT, I focus on this one thing: Forgetting the past and looking forward to what lies ahead.

Paul, once named Saul, was a fierce persecutor of Christians. He hated them. His job was to go around and stop the spreading of the teaching about Jesus and even to kill those who wouldn't. Then one day Saul, on his way to persecute and kill Christians, was blinded by Jesus on the road to Damascus. Upon that experience Saul's name was changed by God to Paul. He was then converted and became a follower of Jesus. Not just an ordinary follower either. This man spent the remaining years of his life doing all he could to get the message out about Jesus, despite his checkered past. He even went on to plant multiple churches and write 2/3rds of the New Testament. Paul had a past, but God still had a future for him.

It is easy for us to get stuck in the past and believe that because of our mistakes we have somehow forfeit our future. Yet, the same man that once killed Christians writes in the letter to the Philippian church, that after all he has done, been through, and has happened to him, "I focus on this one thing: Forgetting the past and looking forward to what lies ahead." There is so much to learn from Paul about his trust and faith in God from this one profound verse. We see that Paul understood the grace of God and the heart of humanity. He knew that he would make mistakes, that others would hurt him, that tragedy would take place, but that none of these things were worth shifting his focus from the hope he had in God.

Paul didn't allow his circumstances to determine his course. His course was set regardless of what took place in his life. Paul had seen God move time and time again and knew that He would continue to move as long as his faith remained intact. So, what does Paul do? He forgets about the past. That doesn't mean he actually doesn't remember it at all. That is ridiculous. It means that he doesn't let it take hold of him. He remembers it, remembers the pain, remembers the hurt, remembers everything about it, but he doesn't let it hold him back from his future in Christ.

The issue for us is that we don't see ourselves on the same level as someone like Paul. We struggle to relate with most of the people in the Bible, especially the writers because if they are in the Bible or wrote it, they must have a closer relationship with God. Yet, that is simply not true. Every person mentioned in the Bible had their own struggles. Every one of the writers were human. They all had their own will that was opposite of God's will until they came to the knowledge of worshiping Him. But at that moment of commitment to worship God, every Bible character immediately fell under the grace God provides for repented hearts. That means that you and I are the same as the people in the Bible and the writers. We are all human in need of a God to save us. Since that is the overall governing truth, we no longer have to fall to the lie that God cannot do in us what He did in them. We can now live just like Paul did. Forgetting what lies behind us and press on to the hope in God before us. We don't have to be dominated by our past mistakes. We can release the guilt we carry from the divorce. We can forget about the pain the past brought. Not forgetting as if to never remember it again, but as to have no hold on your present or future because it doesn't have to.

The truth is you can trust God. I am going to say that again. You can trust God. I know things have happened in life that may challenge your understanding of God, but it doesn't mean you cannot trust Him. He is worthy to be trusted, and the only one that will actually keep His promises. You may wonder, "How is God keeping His promises when He allowed me to go through a divorce?" I think you may be missing the reality that God did not cause the divorce even though He allowed it. The divorce was caused by the dissatisfaction of a deceitful human heart that led one or both of you down a path to where the marriage was severed. But that doesn't make it God's fault or mean that He can't be trusted.

The fact that you are alive, still here, and able to read this book should if nothing else reignite the flame that maybe God isn't totally against you. That would be a good start. Then begin the process of forgiving yourself and others so that you can take your focus off those things and place your focus back on God. It is not about forgetting the past, but remembering it, and allowing forgiveness to be the new lenses you look back through rather than resentment. Don't stay stuck in this place of hoping for the past to come back when God is moving you to a new normal. One that comes with new joys, new experiences, new people, and a renewed faith, hope, and love for the God that you now have begun to trust.

No matter how long I live or what happens in my life, I will never forget the impact 9/11 had on me. It is forever intertwined with my childhood. I cannot just blot it out, and act like it never happened. I can recall the videos of the planes crashing into the twin towers as if it had only happened yesterday. Many people around the world share that same experience and because of that, we all live differently. Things changed that day, and so did we. The same is true for us that have been through a divorce. We will never forget that experience, and we weren't meant to. Instead, we should accept what took place by recognizing that we cannot change the past, but we can change the future.

CHAPTER SEVEN GROWTH PLAN

1. What piece of your tomorrow are you still holding on to? What areas of your life have you taken back from God?

2. Meditate on Matthew 6:19-34. Listen to the words of Jesus. Hear His heart for humanity to relinquish control, and begin to trust in God again. What areas of your life is God telling you to let go of?

3. Are you prone to trying to forgive and just forget? If so, why? How can you begin to "Forget Forward"?

4. Mediate on Philippians 3:10-14. Listen to what Paul is actually saying about how he has overcome those things that try to hold him back. Make a list of things God has revealed to you that might be holding you back from experiencing Him.

5. What will your new normal look like?

CHAPTER EIGHT:

THE SEARCH FOR INTIMACY

Have you ever gone out shopping for something you really wanted but couldn't find it? So then instead of being patient and waiting for what you really want you get something similar. It could be a shirt you really wanted, and you find it, but it's just a different color. You really wanted the red shirt, but you will settle for the brown. If you are like me, it's shoes. I love shoes. Some may say I have an unhealthy obsession with shoes. I would argue against that person and say I have a passion for them. Anyway, there have been times that I have gone out with the intention to buy a pair of shoes that I really wanted. I have the colors picked out. I am even planning my future outfits with them. Weird, I know. What I am saying is I am excited. Then I get to the store, see the shoes on the rack, get the employee to help find my size, only to be told they don't have them. Those words, "we don't have your size," have always been a gut punch.

What happens next is the same thing that happens to many of us. They don't have what we came for, so we will settle for something similar. We will settle for something that brings us the same excitement of getting something new. You shoppers know exactly what I am talking about. There is nothing like coming home with something new after shopping, even if it isn't what you were originally searching for. Then one of two things happen when you buy the item you bought because of your lack of patience. It either gets put in the closet or on the shelf only to be worn a few times. Then when you look at it, it is a constant reminder of the mistake you made buying it. Or you just get rid of it all together after a few wears, only to go back and try to find what you originally wanted. This actually happens more often than not. People settle in all areas of life. It is because when we are searching for something, we are putting our hopes in that one thing to bring us some type of temporary joy or satisfaction in the moment. When what we are searching for is not there, we still need our fix so we don't just leave empty handed, we leave with something to achieve that feeling we came for.

Something similar can happen to us during and after the divorce. Except the thing we are searching for is not a piece of clothing on a rack or a pair of new shoes. In this season we are searching for something much more. Something that we hope to fill a much larger hole in our being. We are searching for intimacy. We are searching for someone to come alongside us and fill that void. We are begging on the inside for that same love and affection we lost. We are searching for that light of hope among the looming darkness of thoughts and fears of loneliness. We all want intimacy. It is how we were designed. We are intimate beings. Intimacy is not the problem, it is actually the solution. The problem is that we often substitute the real intimacy we need for a convenient, temporary "in stock at the moment" intimacy.

That is what often leads you back into relationships that become even more unhealthy than the one you just got out of. We find ourselves even more hurt and lonelier because we allowed the devastation of divorce to cloud our vision of true intimacy. We have diluted it down to someone that will say nice things, allow us physical pleasure, and make us feel good for a little while. Until we recognize we substituted our need for intimacy with something second best. This is the dangerous side of divorce that we must be watching out for. Your search for intimacy is valid, but where you are searching may not be the best location.

The Intimacy You Don't Need

Our go to for intimacy is people. It is in our DNA to desire intimacy, but the source of it cannot be a person. Yet, the world tells us that is where it comes from, and we have bought into that lie over and over again. That is why we see more divorced Christians praying for another husband or another wife more than we see them praying for more of God. We love God but in that moment we think God wants us happy, and the way He brings us to happiness is by giving us what we want. I am sorry to be the bearer of bad news but God's desire for you is not to be happy. His desire is for you to be Holy (1 Peter 1:15-16). When we settle for happiness over holiness, we are settling for second best. Because we have bought into this lie that God just wants us to be happy, so we try to bring about that happiness on our own in the form of another relationship and in the name of God. However, what if I told you that the way you will find happiness is through Holiness?

What if I told you that God doesn't desire for you to have a new spouse for intimacy, but a new source for intimacy? Well, both of those statements are true. God desires you to have a new source of intimacy, which is Him. Through intimacy with God, you will find yourself to be more like Him. You will begin to become Holy like Him. Then you will find happiness in Him, and you won't have to settle for second best when you find yourself searching. You can go straight to the source and always be filled up! The reason we find ourselves seeking intimacy in all the wrong places is not just because we are missing the presence of another person in our life, it is because we are missing the presence of God in our lives. I will be the first to tell you, this was my greatest struggle. It took me years to begin to understand, and today I still feel I am barely scratching the surface. But I can honestly say, switching my attention from seeking intimacy from others to seeking it from God, has radically changed my outlook on what people can actually give me. I've realized that nobody can give me what God can give me. Nobody can give me the love I desire like God can. Nobody can tell me the words I desire to hear like God can. Nobody can listen to my cries like God can. Nobody can heal my hurt like God can. I just wish I wouldn't have wasted so much time going to others when God was there the whole time. I wish that I wouldn't have spent all those days and nights settling for second best. That is why I am telling you now, God's intimacy is always "in stock." He is a one stop shop for all intimacy. He is a one size fits all God. The problem is not with God. It is with our lack of time spent with Him.

Intimacy With God Through Prayer

I wish I could say I immediately got this right when I was going through a divorce, but I didn't. I found myself trying to fill my intimacy bucket with people, and not with prayer, which only left me more empty than I was when I started. The truth is we desire physical and emotional relationships. We want someone to tell us nice things about us. We want people to care about us. We want people to like us. We want someone to tell us they love us and mean it! Well, I have good news for you! God can do all those things. Not only can He but He wants to. Did you know that God genuinely wants to be the source of your intimacy? He wants to surround you with His presence in such a way that you physically feel Him with you. He wants to hear about all your problems and heal your broken heart. He wants to tell you how much He loves you and how amazing you are to Him.

God desires all these things, but we have to be willing to meet Him halfway. That means we have to be willing to pray! I know, what some of you are thinking, *I need to pray more? I pray all the time.* Others may be thinking, *Well, I try to pray but I just don't really know how.* Well to the first group, I am not saying you don't pray. What I am saying is that we must learn how to pray bold and effective prayers. We have to go beyond praying for the laundry list of needs we have. To the second group, prayer is a conversation with God, and I am going to share with you some tips on how to have that conversation. For both groups, let me give you my personal prayer outline. I follow what I call the "3 Ps of Prayer".

> **PRAISE** - I praise God for who He is. Regardless of what I am going through, God is still God. He is still the author of life and deserves to be praised. Therefore, we should start every prayer with a moment of praise.
>
> **PROCLAIM** - I proclaim God's will for my life over my wants for my life. It is easy to fall victim to asking God for things you want rather than being open and accepting what he may have willed for you. If you only accept what you want in your life, then you will close yourself off to the will of God. So, it is important to keep His will for your life at the center of your prayers.
>
> **PLEAD** - I plead for my needs. After I give God honor and ask for His will to be done. I plead for

the things that are on my heart. I ask God for what I need while keeping an open heart and mind to how He may supply those needs. I plead to Him understanding that He wants to hear from me. At the same time, I accept that His timing and techniques might be different than what I expect.

Understanding that God wants to hear from us, but we also have to accept how He chooses to answer us can be a mental battle in and of itself. As we want God to answer our prayers exactly as we pray them, He might just have other plans. That means we don't go to God because we hope that our words will appeal to Him in a way that He will instantaneously fix our problems exactly how we asked. That is not how God works. God is not a genie in a bottle. As a matter of fact, there is one prayer you don't need to be praying right now that many of you, including myself, have fallen guilty of praying. That prayer is, "God get me out of this." Let me let you in on a little secret. A prayer like that does nothing for you and brings no glory to God.

Think about it. If God acted as your genie in a bottle, you would never have a need for Him until you were in trouble. As a matter of fact, you could live however you wanted and then once you were in trouble, you could call on God like a lawyer showing up to get you out of a bind. But a relationship like that is no relationship at all. There is no intimacy involved. So, what should your prayer be? Not, "God get me out of this." But instead, "God help me through this."

When you begin to pray this prayer, it changes everything. "God help me through this" is a bold and powerful prayer that will show its effectiveness daily. When you pray this prayer, you are saying, "God no matter how bad it is, no matter how much it hurts, no matter the circumstances I am facing, I am inviting you into the middle of it all."

That is a prayer that shows the world the love, grace, and mercy of God. How magnificent and infinite in wisdom is the God we serve? To think that He would not just pull us out of the mess as if we were a nuisance to Him, but that He would come into our mess and walk with us on a daily basis because we are that important to Him. Did you realize you are that important to God? He wants to walk with you through the mess. It is happening whether you like it or not, but will you invite God in on it, or resent Him for not pulling you out of it? Your need for intimacy starts with praying the right prayer, but it doesn't stop there.

Intimacy with God through His word

We have heard it said that prayer is a conversation with God. That is true. The problem with most of our prayer life is that we dominate the conversation. We spend much of the time telling God what we need, when we need it, and why we need it. But how many times do we go to God asking for *more of Him* and not just *more from Him*? How often do we go to God to listen and not speak? I bet that is a tough one. For some, you have never even considered silence as part of the prayer. Let me give you another mind blowing idea: how about reading God's word for prayer? Think about it. If prayer is a conversation between us and God, how does God speak to us? I'll tell you how. Through His word. Better known as, *The Bible*.

The greatest way to have a conversation with God is by letting Him start the conversation through the reading of His word. If you want to know what God has to say about the crisis you are dealing with right now, stop talking and start listening. Do you really think God doesn't know what you are going through or what you are feeling? I can assure you that He does. The issue is not with God's lack of communication, but our lack of listening to Him. When we don't understand how the prayer conversation works with God, we miss out on the most important voice in the conversation, God's. So, if you desire true intimacy with God through prayer, start by reading His word.

One common thing I find a lot of people saying is that they just don't hear from God. With all due respect, it's not a God problem, it's a you problem. The people that say they are not hearing from God are not going to the place where He has left the greatest voice recording of all time, the Bible. All the words we need to hear from God have already been recorded and compiled in one place called the Bible. The problem is not with God but with us. The truth is the majority of Christians just flat out don't read the Bible. They go to church. They may even serve. Heck, I bet they might even pray a prayer or two. But as for reading the word of God, that rarely happens. I believe the reason this happens is because we have bought into the lie that the Bible is "hard" to read. Maybe you were like me and one time you picked up a King James Version of the Bible, read a line or two, and then put it down because of the outdated language.

The good news is that there are so many better versions today that are much easier to read so that cannot be an excuse any longer. I always tell people that if they would just read the Bible as a story, it would be much easier to read. Instead, we approach it like some mystical book that has some secret sequences of words that only priests and preachers can understand. However, that is not true at all. The Bible is the greatest love story ever written of God for His creation. If you desire to hear from God, then you have to read His word.

The Search For Intimacy

In order to divorce divorce and live with real intimacy, you have to get this part right. Prayer and reading the Bible have to become a priority. Not just praying for what you need or going to verses for comfort. Instead, it is praying and reading out of necessity to survive. When prayer and the word of God become your source of intimacy with God, they become the spring of water that keeps you alive in Him. When you have tasted the sweet spirit of God falling upon you during a session of crying out for more of Him and not more from Him, you will understand what true intimacy in prayer is like. When you have had your heart filled with the unconditional love of God simply by reading His word, you will never be the same again. Nothing in this world will ever match those two sources of intimacy. I am inviting you to stop going to those empty wells of intimacy and come to the well that never runs dry. That is Jesus Christ.

CHAPTER EIGHT GROWTH PLAN

1. Take a moment and list all the things you do, good or bad, to fill the void of intimacy in your life. What things do you do that you need to stop doing?

2. How would you describe your prayer life? Is it talking to God or listening to God? What area do you need to improve on?

3. Take a moment and sit in complete silence. During this time, reflect on the things your heart desires most. I.e. Love, companionship, etc. Then, listen for God to speak to your heart about how He can provide all those things.

4. Write down two names of individuals of the same sex that you can share your struggles and needs for intimacy with as an act of accountability.

5. Create a plan of action for daily time with God. Your plan should include:

    A. Reading the word of God
    B. Listening to the word of God
    C. Praying for more of God

CHAPTER NINE:

DON'T FORFEIT

I played football from the time I was nine years old until my senior year of high school. I loved football. Not so much the practice but the games. I think anybody that ever played any sport would say the same thing. I would look at the schedule every week just waiting with anxious anticipation to get on the field. When game day came, it was the highlight of the week. I would often wear my jersey to school to let everyone know that I played football, and that it was gameday. One day, after coming home from school, I was getting ready for my afternoon game. Running around the house making sure I had all my equipment ready to go when my dad got home. This day was different though. It was the day I heard a word I hadn't heard before. My dad came in and told me that we didn't have a game that night because the other team had to forfeit. Unfortunately, they didn't think they had enough players to play, so they accepted the loss and didn't make the trip to play. They allowed the idea that they may not have enough players to determine if they would show up or not. The odds were not in their favor, so they forfeited the game.

As I am reminded of that story, I think to myself, how many of us let divorce be the driving factor behind the things that we forfeit in life. Like when I see parents forfeit being a good example for their children by ripping their spouse apart with words their children have never heard. All of this while telling them to be nice to others at school and to say nice things. Or when I see the loneliness of divorce drive someone to forfeit their self-control. To the point that they find themselves self-medicating with pills, drinks, or even with other human intimacy. Or worst of all, when I see someone completely walk away from God and forfeit their faith. Claiming that God could have and should have stopped this from happening. The truth is, wounds from divorce only cut deeper and stay longer when you let divorce cause you to forfeit things in life. In this chapter I want to talk about a couple of the things I myself and others forfeit most during divorce that later causes so much pain. Let this chapter be a warning as you process your divorce.

Don't Forfeit Your Relationship with Your Children

Maybe you don't have children. I don't have them, but as I write it, I am writing as a simple observer. I hope to help others with kids. I invite you in to read as an observer. Maybe you have friends or family in the same situation but with kids. Let this be a guide to help you.

I remember when I was first exposed to the word divorce. I was a young boy at a little league baseball game when a man decided to bring his new girlfriend to watch his son play. I don't know if he knew his ex-wife would be there or not but needless to say, she was not happy. Long story short, an argument ensued that led to me asking my parents what this word "divorce" meant. As they explained I remember being terrified. The idea that moms and dads would actually separate. That kids would have to go live in different homes. Or even the possibility that they may have a new mom or dad come into their lives someday. I couldn't imagine how moms and dads could all of a sudden say they don't love each other anymore. In my young mind, I had not yet understood marriage or the depths and the hurt some parents carried. So, for me, this was a foreign concept. Yet, an all too familiar reality for a lot of children. Not just that their parents are getting divorced, but now they somehow have found themselves to be right smack in the middle of it. Like a rope in a game of tug of war on the playground. They feel as though they are being ripped apart into two different directions by two people that once were the ones that would hold them together. Now they feel like they are the ones trying to hold on to both parents by giving slack to one for a while and then giving slack to the other. Meanwhile, the child is the one standing in the mud the whole time.

Being in ministry for so long, and now a pastor of a church, I see it more times than I would have ever hoped. The worst part of a divorce for me is watching how children become used in the process over the years. Whether it is a child used as the rope in their parents' game of tug of war over who has rights to what, or a child that has been asked to choose between mom or dad. I have seen children with no voice constantly being used as tokens, held by one spouse or the other as a threat to the point that one parent, or both, no longer value the child for being their child. Instead, they use the value of their child to exploit their spouse into doing what they want.

If you are reading this, I want you to understand something. Your children are not tokens! You know it is not your child's fault. However, when a child is used as a tool to benefit one spouse or the other, they begin to believe that whatever happened between mom and dad, must have something to do with them. No matter what is happening in your divorce remember this, children, innocent bystanders, are never to become the casualties of a war that should have never started. That is the fast track to forfeiting your relationship with them in the future. Simply because of pride, bitterness, and manipulation.

You may be reading this section thinking, "I feel like I have forfeited my relationship with my children. What should I do?" Well, there is good news. Just like God redeemed a sinful humanity to himself, He can redeem a child to his or her parents. This will take time, transparency, and forgiveness. This is also part of the process of divorcing divorce that will require self-reflection, and a whole lot of grace. Don't continue to forfeit your relationship with your children because you have been known to do it in the past. Seek God for forgiveness, seek your children for forgiveness, and seek your ex-spouse for forgiveness if necessary. Do whatever it takes to redeem the relationship and restore your example. God doing whatever it took sent His son to the cross. Think about that. What are you sacrificing to stop forfeiting? What have you allowed to get in the way of your relationship with your children that you are willing to go through heaven and hell to redeem, like God did for you?

Don't Forfeit Your Self-Control

This was a hard one for me. I thought I had self-control until I found myself with all new freedoms, and no one to hold me accountable. After losing my wife and my job, I had a season where I forfeited my self-control. Meaning I literally stopped utilizing one of the fruits (or powers) of the Holy Spirit promised to me by God when He saved me. I hope you realize that when you come to Jesus you no longer have to pray for the fruits of the Spirit. Things like patience, kindness, gentleness, and self-control, just to name a few. The Bible says they are things that come naturally with the Holy Spirit, and the salvation of our

Spirit being sealed in Christ. The problem is that God also gives us free will. With that, sometimes we forfeit when it comes to utilizing the fruits God has given us. We tend to fight against the fruits instead of trying to digest them, even when we know they are good for us. Like a child having to eat a fruit they don't like with their meal, instead of eating it, they push it aside. We do that with the fruits God has given us. If it is hard to stomach, we don't.

When it comes to going through divorce, forfeiting self-control can lead us to a far worse situation than just divorce. It can lead to a lifestyle of sexual gratification to fill the void of loneliness. You went from a stable marriage, where you felt safe, pure, love, and consistency with the one you love. Then you forfeit your self-control once, and then twice, and then again. Eventually, you don't even care about the damage you have done to yourself. The morals you once had become a little looser, but the hole of loneliness just gets deeper. You never saw yourself like this when you were at the altar saying, "I do." So, you question what has happened to you. It started with divorce and then ended with forfeiting your self-control to fill a void only Jesus can fill. But it is not just sex. That is just one form of self-medication to try to achieve the feeling of normalcy again in life. Although normalcy is not on the other side of loose morals, only more pain and hurt.

Another area we must be careful not to forfeit our self-control is in substance abuse. For me, this led to years of alcohol dependence. Although I would not classify myself as an alcoholic, I had struggled as an addict before, so alcohol became my "legal" way of coping. With that, it didn't take long to forfeit my self-control. It started slowly, lasted a long time, and came to an abrupt end that took a lot of humility. From start to finish there were many years of hurt in between. I wish I could say this was not part of my story but it was. I forfeited my self-control to a bottle of liquor. I sought it more than Jesus to restore my heart. I ran to it more than the Bible to hopefully quench my thirst. I would literally tell myself, I was in control, but I wasn't. The truth is, when you forfeit your self-control, you give control to something else. For me it was substance abuse through alcohol.

Maybe you have found yourself forfeiting self-control. It could be in one of the few topics we mentioned, or you could have your own problem of self-medication that forces you to forfeit self-control. The number one reason we forfeit our self-control is for temporary pleasures. What temporary pleasure are you going to? What temporary pleasure has become the one thing that makes you go against the Spirit of self-control you know that God placed inside of you when Christ saved you? Here is some good news. You may have forfeited in certain areas of your life, but God has never forfeited on you. You may have quit some days, but God never quit on you. You don't have to live your life forfeited anymore. You don't have to quit when things get hard. You don't have to continue to hurt your relationship with your kids. It is not too late to go back and let God restore what you have lost. You don't have to continue to give in to the addictions and false senses of gratification in your life. You don't have to forfeit your self-control anymore.

Don't Forfeit Your Faith

I have yet to figure this part out, but I have seen it in almost every "Christian Divorce." That is to say, divorce among Christian families. Here is what I observe: I see a Christian get divorced, and then it is like they are not a Christian anymore. Can I just say, it's very confusing already to the world that

Divorcing Divorce

Christians are going through divorce, but even more confusing when they lose their religion in the process. There have been strong Christian men and women throughout history getting a divorce for whatever reason, only to forfeit their example of living a life of Christ in the face of unforeseen trouble.

The book of James in the Bible tells us that we should rejoice through all trials and tribulations. He is not saying that to rejoice in the fact that you are going through a divorce. But he is pointing to a group of people that are hurt, alone, and are struggling with forfeiting their faith, toward the hope of a God that loves them, wants to redeem them, and reminds them that they are not alone. If you are going through a divorce, I know that you are facing all three of those feelings. You are hurt. You feel alone. You have even questioned your faith. I also know that you need to be pointed to the truth that your heart will be held: you are not alone, and God still loves you! Read Romans 8:35-39, NLT. The Bible reads:

> 35 Can anything ever separate us from Christ's love? Does it mean he no longer loves us if we have trouble or calamity, or are persecuted, or hungry, or destitute, or in danger, or threatened with death? 36 As the Scriptures say, "For your sake we are killed every day; we are being slaughtered like sheep." 37 No, despite all these things, overwhelming victory is ours through Christ, who loved us. 38 And I am convinced that nothing can ever separate us from God's love. Neither death nor life, neither angels nor demons, neither our fears for today nor our worries about tomorrow—not even the powers of hell can separate us from God's love. 39 No power in the sky above or in the earth below—indeed, nothing in all cre-

Don't Forfeit

ation will ever be able to separate us from the love of God that is revealed in Christ Jesus our Lord.

Can I just remind you that this verse applies to divorced people too? You have not been separated from the love of God, so don't forfeit your faith based on feelings that are only temporary. Do not forfeit your example to others of God's steadfast love for you based on lies from the devil. Do not forfeit your testimony and the testimony God is building in the midst of this temporary tragedy. Let this trial become your testimony. Don't forfeit your faith before allowing God to make your mess into a miracle. He will use everything you are going through for good if you will let Him. So, if you feel like you have slipped when it comes to your faith, you don't have to continue slipping. God desires you to put your faith back in Him. Call out to Him today. He loves hearing from His children!

You may feel as though you have given up on God, but the good news is that God never gave up on you. Even in the time you gave up on yourself. He has always been right there ready to receive you. It is time to stop forfeiting things in life so that you can stop living in the guilt and shame that Christ has already covered by His blood on the cross. When you stop forfeiting and start fighting, you will begin to divorce divorce. Not just the identity of divorce, but all the negative feelings you have about yourself that forfeiting in the process made you feel. Are you ready to stop quitting and start trusting in God?

CHAPTER NINE GROWTH PLAN

1. Do you see an area that you have forfeited or been tempted to in the process of your divorce?

2. What are some steps you can take to make sure that you don't forfeit in any area?

3. When you feel like forfeiting, who do you talk to? Have you been honest with them?

4. How does it make you feel to know that God has never quit on you?

5. How does knowing God's love for you help you to keep going?

CHAPTER TEN:

HOPE IN THE RIGHT HANDS

I grew up in a small town called Pendleton, South Carolina. If you aren't looking for it you wouldn't know if you passed through it. Growing up in a small town means that we have our lives mapped out at a young age. And all maps lead to the same place. To marriage. It doesn't matter whether or not your map includes getting a job after high school or going to college. It doesn't matter if it includes staying in your small town or getting out. Every map leads to the same "treasure," where love is the "x" that marks the spot. That treasure is called marriage. Everybody has hopes and dreams of getting married. Everybody wants to share their life with somebody. I am sure mapping out your life isn't just a small town thing. I would imagine the same is true for you regardless of where you grew up. That means we all are faced with the same dilemma when we finally reach our goal of marriage. What is next?

For many of us marriage has been seen as a finish line and not a starting place. Because of that, when we get to the finish line only to get divorced, all our hopes are gone. We have wasted so much time and energy that we don't want to run that race again only to get to the finish line and fail again. The problem is not so much the race or pursuit of marriage. The problem is that marriage has been taught to be the "goal". When marriage is the goal, it becomes our hope. Everything we do in life is to lead us to that moment. To that altar where we get to kiss our bride or our groom and give our lives to each other only to live happily ever after. But what happens when that doesn't happen? What do you do when all you had ever hoped for seems to have slipped through your fingers? What happens when you place your whole life in the hands of another under that covenant of marriage, only to be dropped like a basket of eggs shattering your very existence? I'll tell you what happens. You have to put your hope in the right hands. You have to put your hopes back in the hands of God.

When I think about what it looks like to put our hopes in the hands of God, I am reminded of the story of a woman in the Bible whose name you may not recognize. The woman's name is Jochebed. After nine months of a grueling pregnancy Jochebed gave birth to a son. What should have been a day of joy was actually a day of terror. The Pharaoh had decreed a death sentence to all newborn Hebrew male babies. This decree caused Jochebed to hide her child for three months. She held onto the hope that she could protect her child. Until the day came that she could hide him no longer. After risking her entire family's life for so long she was forced to do the unthinkable. Give up total control of her child, putting her hope in a wicker basket and reeds in a river.

But was that really where her hope was? Or was her hope finally in the hands of God? I would argue that her hope was in God. As she remembered upon the story of Noah, she made an ark like structure to protect her child from the water he would have to endure. As she went down to the river it was finally time to take her hands off the situation completely and put her hopes in God. I like to say that she finally had her "Hopes up and Hands up." It is easy for us to have hopes up and hands on, but here we see the opposite. She put her hopes up in God, and her hands off the situation. We see her faith paid off when an Egyptian girl, who happened to be the Pharaoh's daughter, found the baby in a basket and decided to preserve his life. This woman who placed her hope for her son's life in the hands of God is none other than the mother of Moses, one of the greatest men of the Bible.

I couldn't imagine how hard that would have been to have to leave my child in a river and hope that God preserves his life. She could have continued to hope in her own abilities but then she risked the child dying. Could you imagine the Bible without Moses? I can't. I think this is a great example of what it looks like to truly put your hope in God. The problem for many of us is that we grew up with the "American Dream" of marriage in mind and without realizing it our hope for our lives was placed in our hands and not God's hands. We already had our lives planned. We didn't need to put our lives in God's hands.

We think we just need to have faith in Him, but we can place our hopes in things we can control. That is a protection mechanism against pain at its core. You may or may not realize it but when your whole life culminates in this idea of happily ever after with another human being, your hopes are destined to be shattered. If you are reading this, you already know. Your hope was never meant to be put in the hands of another person, in a marriage, or in an idea of happily ever after. Your hope is meant to be placed in Christ and Christ alone. The truth is, Christ is the only one strong enough to hold our hopes, but all too often we put our hopes in the wrong hands. I believe that is why divorce hurts so much. Somewhere along the way the marriage became the mission and then it became our God. Our entire identity became wrapped up in our husband or our wife.

Hope In The Right Hands

We loved to be known by how happy we were, by how big our house was, by how nice our cars were, and even how well our kids did academics or sports. Then one day we wake up to have our lives ripped apart by the reality of divorce.

All of a sudden, your hope came crashing down like a house of cards because the place you kept them was unstable. This is an all familiar reality for most of us. I know my hopes were in my newly purchased, big, two-story house. I mean for all intents and purposes I had made it. My dreams were a reality. I had a wife. I had a dream job. I had a beautiful home. I had it all, from the outside looking in. But the truth is my kingdom was built on the sand. All that I had placed my hopes in were things that were not eternal. That is why I spiraled so far so fast when all of it was being ripped away. My fear is that many of you have made the same mistake. You feel like you are drowning in a place with no hope because your hope was placed in a ship that sank. So, what are you supposed to do now? Let me help you. Hope in the right hands. Stop hoping in the hands of the world and begin hoping in the hands of the Father. This world has nothing for you. No amount of money, relationships, cars, houses, or any other earthly possession has the capacity to uphold your hope. The only hands strong enough to hold you and all of your hopes are the hands of Jesus.

As a Christ follower for several years and a minister of the Gospel, it can be hard to imagine that my hope wasn't always in the solid rock of Jesus Christ. Well, it wasn't. Like many Christians, I loved Jesus. I had a strong relationship with Him. However, I lost my way and began putting my hopes in the wrong hands. I tell you this because if you are feeling hopeless, it is because your hope is in the wrong hands. The good news is that God is still on the throne and still in control. His character is not determined by your mistakes; you can still go to Him. As a matter of fact, He is waiting for you to come to Him. He is waiting for you to finally stop putting your hopes in another idol that will help you to forget about your divorce and numb the pain.

Instead, He invites you to come to Him. He welcomes you back into His loving arms to be your hope in this world. He is truly all you need. As you divorce divorce you also start putting your hope in the right hands again. Not the temporal hands of this world, but the eternal hands of our loving Father in Heaven, Jesus Christ.

CHAPTER 10: GROWTH PLAN

1. Was marriage the "goal" for you growing up? If so, how has your mindset changed?

2. What hopes did you place on your marriage?

3. List any and all areas of life that you feel hopeless in today.

4. How can you make sure you are placing your hope in God and not the world?

5. Write out a prayer to God asking Him to be the hands in which your hopes are held.

CONCLUSION

The vivid memory of the day I sent the text in the chapel to the day I received the text that the unthinkable was happening will forever be in my mind. There are just some things that we can't forget. However, none of the things that happened to me during and after my divorce hold me captive any longer. I can honestly say I have divorced the identity of being divorced. It rarely crosses my mind, and the pain I once felt no longer plagues my heart and my mind. I know for someone reading this right now that day seems to be years away. Can I encourage you? That day of healing has already begun. You may not feel it. You may not see it. You may not even realize it is happening until it happens. But the truth that you are leaning into God and making decisions to divorce divorce, the healing is already beginning.

The reality that we can't forget about is that all healing is a process that we must endure. It takes time and patience but along the way you will begin to see the healing hand of God at work. You will begin to feel the detachment of the identity you have adopted. You will begin to feel your identity in Christ being restored. Just make sure you don't give up in the process. That is the only thing that will stop you from divorcing divorce and reclaiming your life in Christ. The devil is always at work and will try anything he can to make you give up along the way. However, those who trust in God will make it through to the other side.

I never expected to be divorced. I think all divorcees would say the same thing. It wasn't part of our master plan for our lives. If you would have told me when I was younger that I would end up divorced, like many of you, I would have said you were crazy. I knew what I wanted out of life and divorce was never an option. Yet, life happens to all of us. Daily decisions are made that slowly but surely affect the overall outcome of our lives and especially our marriages. That is how it happened for me and for you. Decisions were made that led to circumstances to which there was no coming back. To this day, the fact that I have been divorced is still something that shocks me back to reality when I meet someone else that has had the same experience. I will say that the feelings and emotions of going through a divorce do get better over time. But only when you make the conscious decision to divorce your divorce. That means you no longer let the devil hold you back in this place of unworthiness. As if you are a failure that has gone beyond redemption. Instead, you claim and cling to the victory that you have in Christ Jesus on a daily basis. Never forgetting that His love for you far outweighs your failures in Him. You do not have to stay in this defeated state of mind. You can continue to live and even grow stronger through this experience.

It has almost been a decade since I went through my divorce. It took over half of that time to finally overcome it. The feelings of shame and guilt that came with a failed marriage loomed over my existence for a long time. It plagued my reality and my relationships. Part of my divorcing divorce was writing this book and sharing my experience with the world. People will ask, "why write a book exposing yourself like this?" The only answer I have is that I had to. I had to write of my experience in order to shed a small light of hope to the one that finds themselves at the end of their rope, battling the devil, fighting the identity crises,

Conclusion

and praying for new hands to hope in. I had to share my struggles so that others can see what God can do when you allow Him to take total control of your life and restore you to the person He has called you to be.

As I sit here today, I am a happily married man, again, but this time with my hopes fully in Christ. My wife and I moved from South Carolina a few years ago to Miami, FL where we planted a new church called Village Church. Just like I wouldn't have believed you if you would have told me when I was young that I would be divorced, I wouldn't have believed you just a few years ago if you told me God could use me despite my divorce. However, I am living proof that He can. I am living proof that God still has a purpose for your life. I am living proof that your divorce does not have to define you. I am living proof that life is so much more than the season you are currently living. I am living proof that God can take your mess and turn it into a message. So, are you up for the challenge of *Divorcing Divorce*?

FINAL RECAP

1. What chapter resonated with you the most? Why?

2. How have your views of divorce changed or been challenged?

3. Has this book changed how you believe God views you? If so, how?

Conclusion

4. How has this book shaped your mindset towards yourself?

5. Who else will you share this new found knowledge with?

Milton Keynes UK
Ingram Content Group UK Ltd.
UKHW020744080724
445166UK00012B/202